LIGHTEN UP
NICHOLAS BROWN &
SAM McCOOL

CURRENCY PRESS
SYDNEY

GRIFFIN
INDEPENDENT

CURRENT THEATRE SERIES

First published in 2016
by Currency Press Pty Ltd,
PO Box 2287, Strawberry Hills, NSW, 2012, Australia
enquiries@currency.com.au
www.currency.com.au

in association with Bali Padda and Griffin Independent

Cataloguing-in-publication data for this title is available from the National Library of Australia website: www.nla.gov.au

Typeset by Dean Nottle for Currency Press.
Cover image shows Sam McCool.
Cover photograph by Johnny Diaz Nicolaidis.
Cover design by Clare Marshall.

Currency Press acknowledges the Traditional Owners of the Country on which we live and work. We pay our respects to all Aboriginal and Torres Strait Islander Elders, past and present.

Contents

Lighten Up was first produced by Bali Padda and Griffin Independent at SBW Stables Theatre, Sydney, on 2 December 2016, with the following cast:

SANDY	Katie Beckett
JOHN GREEN	Nicholas Brown
BRONWYN	Vivienne Garrett
LIVVY / MERLE OBERON / HEATHER	Julie Goss
ANIL / GUILLAUME / MANA / DOCTOR / INDIAN PRESS PERSON 2	Sam McCool
JANELLE / GAV / RECEPTIONIST / RENEE / CITY OF SYDNEY PRODUCER / INDIAN PRESS PERSON 1	Bishanyia Vincent

Producer, Bali Padda
Director and Dramaturg, Shane Anthony
Director's Attachment, Hannah Tonks
Set and Costume Designer, Tobhiyah Stone Feller
Lighting Designer, Christopher Page
Composer and Sound Designer, Busty Beatz
Design Intern, Maeli Cherel
Stage Manager, Lauren Tulloh

CHARACTERS

JOHN GREEN, late 20s–early 30s, Anglo-Indian Australian with brown skin

SANDY, late 20s–early 30s, Indigenous Australian woman with dark brown skin

BRONWYN, 55, John's mother, Anglo-Indian with fair skin

LIVVY, 10, John's little sister, Anglo-Indian Australian with fair skin

DANNO, late 20s, John's best friend, Australian male, caucasian, redhead

JANELLE BURNS, late 20s, John's girlfriend, blonde caucasian Australian

ANIL DIXIT THE THIRD, 40s–50s, male, Indian film director

MERLE OBERON, the ghost of the 1940's Hollywood actress

MANA, 55, Sandy's father, Maori with dark brown skin

GAV, owner of Cockney Convict Walking Tours, Australian, caucasian

HEATHER, 50s, Anglo-Indian woman with dark brown skin

GUILLAUME GUILLOTINE, a French photographer

RECEPTIONIST, 'Bondi Parade' production receptionist

RENEE BROGAN, 45, Executive Producer of 'Bondi Parade', caucasian woman

CITY OF SYDNEY PRODUCER

DOCTOR

INDIAN PRESS PERSON 1

INDIAN PRESS PERSON 2

FANNY & DICKY, two budgerigars

OLIVIA LOOK-ALIKE, a fantasy of Bronwyn's

The play can be performed by six actors, with roles distributed as follows:

Actor 1: JOHN GREEN

Actor 2: SANDY

Actor 3: BRONWYN

Actor 4: LIVVY / MERLE OBERON / DANNO / HEATHER

Actor 5: JANELLE / RECEPTIONIST / OLIVIA LOOK-ALIKE / RENEE / GAV / CITY OF SYDNEY PRODUCER/INDIAN PRESS PERSON 1

Actor 6: ANIL/GUILLAUME/MANA/DOCTOR/INDIAN PRESS PERSON 2

DANNO could be played by an additional actor (Actor 7) and a caucasian male redhead actor could be cast as this role. He would also double up as GAV and CITY OF SYDNEY PRODUCER.

We encourage anyone producing and casting this work to consider performers from diverse backgrounds, including for roles where a character's ethnic or cultural background, age, gender, sexuality or disability need not be specified.

This play went to press before the end of rehearsals and may differ from the play as performed.

ACT ONE

SCENE ONE

JOHN *sits onstage, pumicing his brown skin with a pumice stone. A ouija board is in front of him. He eventually puts the pumice stone on the ouija board.*

JOHN: I call upon the powers that be and ask whatever's up there beyond the Southern Cross to please hear me. I apologise for losing the movable pointer and hope you'll accept this pumice stone as a way to inform me of any guidance. Please, Southern Cross. Help me: I *must* star in 'Bondi Parade'.

SCENE TWO

BRONWYN *enters. She has bleached blonde hair and wears a skin-tight black outfit. She's holding a large postage package.*

BRONWYN: Good. This batch has aloe vera in it. That should work well with the bleach.

> LIVVY *enters. She has a football down her school uniform, pretending to be pregnant, and is holding a small ghetto blaster. She wheels a huge birdcage onstage. It has two budgies in it—* FANNY *and* DICKY. *The abnormally large-sized budgies are humans dressed as budgies wearing budgie smugglers. There is a breeding box attached to the cage.* FANNY *and* DICKY *do an odd interpretative mating dance—but they don't mate.* BRONWYN *hides her package behind her back.*

LIVVY: Come on, Fanny. Get on a move on, Dicky. What song will make you root?

> LIVVY *plays an Olivia Newton-John song on her ghetto blaster.* JOHN *enters. He's wearing a convict outfit.*

JOHN: Mum, can you get me blue contact lenses for my 'Bondi Parade' audition?

LIVVY: Mum …

BRONWYN: Blue? We agreed to only use green ones, darling … goes with our family brand.

JOHN: I need blue.

BRONWYN: Why?

LIVVY: It's not easy being green …

JOHN: If *I* don't get this role in 'Bondi Parade', I'll inject blue paint into my eyes.

BRONWYN: Blue cornea tattoos are so Korean. Go green, darling.

JOHN: Please, Mum. All the cast have blue eyes. I need to look like them.

LIVVY: Mum …

BRONWYN: No, darling, to succeed you must stand out (while fitting in). Green means go. Now go to work.

LIVVY: Mum …

BRONWYN: Whaaaat?! Bloody kids, I feel a pain in my womb!

LIVVY: Don't shout. You'll scare my budgies and then they'll never root. If I can lay an egg … why can't Fanny?

BRONWYN: Ha! Finally I can look forward to being a grand-MILF.

LIVVY: Mum …

JOHN: Mum, why do you have pics of me and Janelle on your laptop?

BRONWYN: Oh. I've found the most amazing website. It's called Genetics Spawn.

JOHN: Porn?

BRONWYN: No. Spawn. Genetics Spawn. If you upload a picture of your-self and another person … it shows you what your children will look like. Your babies with Janelle will be so beautiful, Johnny. Look! So sweet. So fair and lovely.

JOHN: Danno and I are going to a beer garden in Bondi to listen to the Hottest 100 after work.

BRONWYN: Make sure you wear a hat and sunscreen. Have you not got your green contacts in?

JOHN: My eyes are sore. I'll put them on at work.

BRONWYN: Put them on now please. They cost me a fortune. You look so much more handsome with green eyes, darling.

LIVVY: Mum …

JOHN: I want blue.

BRONWYN: You're getting green. Go to your room and put them on now.

JOHN *exits.*

LIVVY: Mum?

BRONWYN: Pain in my womb! Whaaaat?!

LIVVY: So can Ming-Wa, Rosa and Fatima come over to watch 'Bondi Parade'?

BRONWYN: No they cannot. I need the lounge room free.

LIVVY: For what?

BRONWYN: For my aerobics. Did you mess with the remote controls again, Livvy?

LIVVY: No.

BRONWYN: Liar. Pain in my womb. Play disc four for me? Olivia Newton-John's *Greatest Hits Volume Two.*

LIVVY: Can I watch the ep of 'Bondi Parade' that I set the timer for yesterday?

BRONWYN: You've got school, Livvy. Besides—it's O.N.J. time. Olivia Newtown-John. Turn it on. Do it. Xanadu-it.

LIVVY: So, can Ming-Wa, Rosa and Fatima come over to watch 'Bondi Parade' this arvo?

BRONWYN: Oh, Livvy, isn't one foreign friend enough?

LIVVY: Mum. Ming-Wa's Burmese. Rosa's Panamanian and Fatima's a Lebanese Jew. But they're all born here.

BRONWYN: Stop fabricating foreigners, darling. No such thing as a Lebanese Jew.

LIVVY: Yes there is. I saw it on 'Foreigner Correspondent'.

BRONWYN: Bloody ABC, that's what you get from funding cuts. Trashy TV. Whatever happened to those lovely twins, Karen and Sharon McLaren?

LIVVY: You kicked them out 'cause they were Siamese twins, remember?

BRONWYN That's right. Siamese. Darling, how many times must I tell you, never trust a country that hasn't been colonised. The only Asians you should be mingling with are cauc-asians.

LIVVY: Ming-Ling—oh yeah, I forgot to invite her. She's the new Tibetan exchange student.

BRONWYN: What did they exchange her for? A llama?

LIVVY: I didn't ask Alana … can she come too?

BRONWYN: Alana, now that's more promising. What's her last name?

LIVVY: Riskybitz.

BRONWYN: Is that Jewish?
LIVVY: No, Russian.
BRONWYN: White Russian?
LIVVY: No, black Russian.
BRONWYN: Tell her to bugger off—we're full.

SCENE THREE

JOHN *is searching for his green contact lenses.* MERLE OBERON *crashes on stage in a large puff of powder.*

MERLE: Conceal. Conceal. Conceal.
JOHN: I forgot to take my Xanax.
MERLE: Be thankful I'm even here.
JOHN: What the hell?
MERLE: This isn't a hallucination. I'm here to recruit—I mean to assist you!
JOHN: You are? Do you know where my green contacts are then?
MERLE: Third drawer behind the *Blonde Babes* magazines.
JOHN: Oh. Thanks.
MERLE: Am I in Tasmania?
JOHN: No. You're in Greystanes.
MERLE: Good Lord. Where the hell is that?
JOHN: It's in between Parramatta and Blacktown. Who the hell are you?
MERLE: I helped Cliff Richard top the charts. I suggested Englebert Humperdinck as a stage name … Humperdinck! Pure genius?! But my greatest triumph … I got Ben Kingsley the role of Gandhi.
JOHN: Gandhi, what's that got to do with me?
MERLE: He was one of the world's greatest game changers! I was puzzled by him at the time. So much positive power in a pocket-sized package. Now I must tell the truth for the first time. I'm here to recruit the new Gandhi. If I don't, I'll never pass through. I must find the chosen one!
JOHN: Are you a casting agent?
MERLE: Yes. No. Only half-caste! You're my last chance. My last assignment.
JOHN: Chance of what?
MERLE: You're the tour guide, correct?

JOHN: Only part-time. I'm really an actor.

MERLE: Heed my wisdom, and one day you will be a great star like him—then you'll use pure powder rather than putrid pumice.

JOHN: You're a star?

MERLE: Surely you recognise me, even in this terrible light?

JOHN: Nope.

MERLE: *Dark Angel*. 1935. Academy Award nomination.

JOHN: I'd rather win a Logie.

MERLE: Television. Uggh.

JOHN: It's my favourite medium.

MERLE: I'm your favourite medium. Merle Oberon. Hollywood's forgotten screen siren. What a privilege it is for you to meet me.

JOHN: Merle Oberon.

MERLE: John Green. Right now you're a tour guide. I'm … a spirit guide. We all must play our roles.

JOHN: So you're here to help me?

MERLE: Indeed.

JOHN: Then help me star in 'Bondi Parade'.

MERLE: I love a parade!

JOHN: 'Bondi Parade's an Aussie soap opera.

MERLE: I adore the opera!

JOHN: It's a TV show. My audition's next month. Is that long enough for you to weave your magic?

MERLE: Hmmm.

JOHN: Look, I've got a life-sized framed poster signed by the original cast, my most prized possession … and each star's headshot arranged on the ceiling in the shape of my favourite constellation … the Southern Cross!

MERLE: You don't look like these 'Bondi Parade' actors, do you?

JOHN: What?

MERLE: You don't fit into the Southern Cross, do you?

JOHN: No. I don't. Help me. Humperdinck me.

SCENE FOUR

Australia Day. JOHN *enters, dressed as a convict. He is leading a tour group.*

JOHN: G'day, everyone! 'Appy Australia Day! Welcome to Cockney Convict Walking Tours. I'm Jolly John, your convict tour guide extraordinaire. I don't want to shackle you up and torture you with colonial history, but it's important to know this very spot where the First Fleet of convicts like me arrived two hundred and twenty-eight years ago—

> SANDY, *an Indigenous woman with dark brown skin, interrupts* JOHN.

SANDY: What a load of rubbish.

JOHN: Um. Excuse me. I'm in the middle of a tour here. As I was saying— [*Back to his tour group*] It was right here at Sydney Cove where the first ships—

SANDY: It wasn't here. It was at Botany Bay. Get your facts straight!

JOHN: Most of us convicts barely stole a loaf of bread. And before we knew it—our lives were toast. On this very day, the twenty-sixth of January, Australia was—

SANDY: Don't listen to him, guys. And it wasn't the twenty-sixth, it was the twenty-first. You want the real story? Here are some flyers.

> *She hands out flyers to the audience.*

JOHN: Okay—let's take a ten-minute break. We'll continue the tour then. Fanks, guys. See you in a bit. [*To* SANDY] I don't get paid enough to deal with this crap. You're really rude, you know that. I was doing a show.

SANDY: Your 'facts' are just fiction!

JOHN: I'm pretty sure that the ships first landed here at Circular Quay.

SANDY: All you're doing is regurgitating the Euro version of our history.

JOHN: And that's why we're allowed in Eurovision. 'Cause we're a European colony.

SANDY: You know nothing.

JOHN: No. I'm just a lowly convict.

SANDY: What were you convicted of? Overacting?

JOHN: You should be convicted for over re-acting. Why were you recording me?

SANDY: I'm taking Cockney Convicts down. You shouldn't be allowed to operate. I'm starting a new tour company. We'll be giving historical Indigenous dance tours of The Rocks, and we're telling the real story.

JOHN: Tour guiding? This is our turf. We've been here for twenty years. You're stealing our intellectual property.

SANDY: You stole our actual property.

JOHN: I was in character.

SANDY: You call that a character?

JOHN: My boss says that the script's fully researched and authentic. You're wasting your money. The Rocks doesn't need two tour guide companies.

SANDY: It's not my money. It's sponsored by the City of Sydney.

JOHN: Really? When do you launch?

SANDY: Next month.

JOHN: I doubt you'll get any customers.

SANDY: Game on.

JOHN: Well, happy Australia Day.

SANDY: Happy Independence Day.

JOHN: What?

SANDY: Isn't it Indian Republic Day today?

JOHN: How would I know?

SANDY: While Australia celebrates British arrival, India celebrates their departure. Both on the twenty-sixth of January. Kinda ironic, isn't it?

JOHN: You've lost me.

SANDY: The British government kicked you convicts out of their country to colonise this one. They dumped their crap all over our land. They call it colonisation, more like colonic irrigation. They did it in India too.

JOHN: I'm not Indian.

SANDY: Oh. It's just all of the Indian restaurants in town have been celebrating Independence today.

GAV *enters.*

GAV: John, can I have a word please?

JOHN: Sure, Gav.

GAV: Look, mate, you know I think you're a diamond. It's just—

JOHN: Gav. I know.

GAV: You do?

JOHN: Yeah. This lady just told me. She's starting a—

GAV: Listen, mate, there's no easy way to say this, mate. I'm getting pressured to hire another actor to play the Cockney convict. I'm gonna have to … to …

JOHN: What?

GAV: I really want Cockney Convict Walking Tours to be an authentic and realistic company. Real convicts just wouldn't have looked like you, John. I'm sorry.

JOHN: What about Spyro? He's been playing Captain Cook for years but he's Greek.

GAV: It's different, mate.

JOHN: How?

GAV: Well, he passes as— Look, sorry, mate, but you just don't fit the bill. Convicts didn't look like you do.

JOHN: [*in a Cockney accent*] They might 'ave after six months at sea. Plus at least I sound the part innit?

GAV: Yeah, mate, but the punters were asking how did a chocolate convict end up in Australia?

JOHN: I've worked here for years, Gav. I really need this job.

GAV: I'm really sorry, John. Today's your last tour of duty. Tell you what, I'll let ya keep your convict costume as a souvenir.

SANDY: Are you gonna let him get away with this?

JOHN: It's a great costume.

SANDY: [*to* GAV] You. Gavin, is it?

GAV: Yeah, who are you?

SANDY: Never you mind. Is this the way you treat your loyal staff?

GAV: Look, I don't know who you think you are, but I don't want any trouble. This is difficult enough as it is.

SANDY: Gavin, hey? Interesting name. Welsh origin. Meaning 'white hawk'. That sounds about right. High-flying predator preying on the innocent. If you don't offer him some sort of retrenchment package, this lady hawk will kick your backside from here to Crows Nest.

GAV: Ah, John … um … if you drop by the office tomorrow, I think we might have some sort of retrenchment package lying around. Sorry again, mate.

SANDY: That's better. Much better.

GAV *exits.*

JOHN: You just Judge Judied him off your turf, Mrs Heckler!

SANDY: I'm still a Miss, thank you, Jolly John.

JOHN: That was amazing! Thank you so much.

SANDY: You're welcome.

JOHN: I can't believe he fired me.

SANDY: Retrenched now.

JOHN: God, I can't believe they called me a chocolate convict. Sounds like an Arnott's biscuit. 'Come and have a cup of tea and a chocolate convict bikky.' I loved those gollywog biscuits.

SANDY: They banned that name. They're called Scallywags now.

JOHN: Can I take you out for a meal? To say thank you?

SANDY: Lunch with a corny, cute convict?

JOHN: You think I'm cute?

SANDY: I think you're corny.

JOHN: I thought you thought I was an overactor.

SANDY: Jim Carrey's an overactor. But he's still hot.

JOHN: So you think I'm hot?

SANDY: I don't even know you. I better head back to work.

JOHN: Hey, thanks.

SANDY: For what?

JOHN: For sticking up for me. No-one ever sticks up for me.

SANDY: I'm sorry about your job. What are you gonna do for work now?

JOHN: I've got an audition for 'Bondi Parade'. It's the best show ever, hey?

SANDY: You're weird.

JOHN: Bondi's the best.

SANDY: Are you from Bondi?

JOHN: No.

SANDY: Where are you from?

SCENE FIVE

BRONWYN *enters and sets up a phone camera to film herself. She presses record.*

BRONWYN: Hi, Olivia. It's me, again. Bronwyn Green. I hope you've been getting these video posts on your fanpage. I wish you'd write back to me. I've been in the front row of all of your concerts in Sydney since the seventies. The merchandise at your last one was just divine. I treasure my O.N.J. clock. It's broken, but reminds me of you: timeless. Olivia. You're the most beautiful person on this planet. Those black pants, O.N.J.! So svelte. I wish I had a figure like yours. My caesareans ruined my waistline. My son still lives at home. My daughter's ten, going on thirty. I named her after you, remember? My son's still unmarried. Such a black sheep. Olivia, when you performed 'I Love a Sunburnt Country' at Expo 88, I had a transcendental experience. I felt so … connected to you. You look so good for your age, Olivia. I hate the way I look! I wish I looked like you. I dyed my hair blonde. Like yours. If I win the lottery, I'll get plastic surgery to look like you. Then maybe you'll respond to me. Let me know when you're in Sydney next and I'll take you for lunch at Greystanes RSL. I love you, Olivia. You've saved me in so many ways. I cried for months when I—

Pause.

When I get migraines, I cry. Your music soothes me. You'd be the best grand-MILF. I just wish you'd respond to my posts. Why won't you acknowledge me? Why are you cruel?! You said on 'Sixty Minutes' that you loved interacting with your fans. Well, I'm your biggest fan and you're a liar, Olivia!

She calms down. She presses stop on her phone.

Damn. I can't post this. Erase. Erase. Delete. Start again.

She presses record again.

Hi, Olivia.

SCENE SIX

DANNO *enters.* JOHN *takes his convict outfit off to reveal shorts and a hypercolour t-shirt. He wraps himself in his towel.*

DANNO: How you going to get discovered, Johnno, if you come to the beach and just sit in the shade?

JOHN: Danno, do you think it'd be a tremendous act of imagination to cast me in 'Bondi Parade'?

DANNO: Not at all. When I'm a famous director I'll cast you in everything.

JOHN: Thanks, man.

DANNO: Dude, since you and Janelle hate Valentine's Day, wanna hang out with me?

JOHN: My audition's on the fifteenth. I have to prep.

DANNO: It's just that it's Ginger Pride Day and I was—

JOHN: There's a Ginger Pride Day? That's hilarious.

DANNO: Why's it hilarious? It's a big global issue now. Redheads get together around the world to march against the adversity we face.

JOHN: I always bashed anyone that teased you, Danno.

DANNO: Will you come with me?

JOHN: Sure! We can go op-shopping and I'll dress up.

DANNO: It's actually more of a dress down thing.

JOHN: What do you mean?

DANNO: Have you ever heard of Guillaume Guillotine? He's a French photographer that travels the world and takes protest photos of large groups of people in major cities naked. He's doing one at Waterloo on V Day for Ginger Pride.

JOHN: Really?

DANNO: We should go and maybe get nude together. You know, for art.

JOHN: I'm into it. Can't stay out too late though,

DANNO: I'm so glad that your agent's finally getting you auditions.

JOHN: She's useless. She's a retired porn actress that makes spiritual erotica.

DANNO: I admire her work.

JOHN: The last audition she wanted me to go for was a film called *Deepak Throat*.

> *Suddenly* ANIL DIXIT THE THIRD, *a tall Indian director, enters. He has a strong Indian accent.*

ANIL: Ladies and gentlemen. Please don't be deterred, I am Anil Dixit … the Third.

DANNO: Right on time.

ANIL: Actually, according to Standard Indian Time, I'm quite early.

DANNO: Mr Dixit. Thank you for squeezing us in. I know you must have a busy schedule.

ANIL: Schedule? I've heard of this useless foreign concept. We Indians prefer organised chaos. [*To an assistant*] Parmeet, we don't need a permit to shoot. I'm not afraid of the local council. Get the cameras ready.

JOHN: Danno—

ANIL: You, you must be Daniel. Now where is this southern star you said I must meet? You got two minutes, my Maggi noodles are cooking.

DANNO: Call me Danno. Anil—this is John Green, your southern star. John—this is—

ANIL: *Mera naam* Anil Dixit the Third. But don't be deterred.

JOHN: I am deterred. I'm outta here.

DANNO: John, he's here shooting a movie.

JOHN: I don't care.

DANNO: My online Pakistani pen pal told me about it.

JOHN: You have a pen pal?

DANNO: Yeah. We play online Scrabble. They speak better English than us, you know.

JOHN: As if.

DANNO: His name's Hasif.

ANIL: Hasif, I have time for all of this *tamasha*! Eh, Baloo, where are my Pali-G biscuits? I can't eat these crappy Scallywags. My glutes are grandiose. From today I go gluten-free. So Bondi.

DANNO: Johnny, Mr Dixit is a big deal, and he's looking for new talent. I thought I'd surprise you and arrange a meeting.

JOHN: This is bullshit, Danno.

DANNO: I thought you'd be excited.

ANIL: *Kya bakwas hai?* I don't have time for this. Kanti, no need for continuity, let's continue the shoot. Bunty, what do you mean you can't swim!? I couldn't care less, you're not in Kerala anymore! Put the shark fin back on, get back in the water. No floaties. You know my policy—no H and S! You're supposed to be a great white, not a wussy wobbygong. Aunty! The koala. Why is he sleeping? We're not paying him to sleep. Wake him up. Sachit—the kangaroo? He's jumping, he's supposed to hop. Hoppity-hop! … Teach him the difference. Hey, Preeti—where are my bikini babes! I need babes! Ooh, not them—we need white girls, with pale translucent skin like a jellyfish, not a glowing orange. Manoj, something's missing. Where's Ashok? Go get Ashok out of his trailer. Wake him gently, you must get Ashok, not him. Quickly, everyone, the light is fading. Sunny, get the fake sun on standby. Ooh, Ashok! You look so dark and roasted! I asked you to slip, slop, slap! Make-up! Wake up! Baby powder for Ashok's face. Think, guys, think! Put on some zinc! Okay, places. Quiet on set. Take two. Lifesavers, go! Lift him. Higher. Hold that move. Keep lifting. Lift him higher. *Arrey*, Ashok—go, son, go. Dancers, pop your pelvis, while you lift him, pop, pop, pop. And move to the water. Leap over the sandcastle. Pop your pelvis. Hold him. Kanti—keep your head in the water! Kanti, hold the shark fin in position. Eh, Speedo boys. Speed up or Kanti will catch you. Don't step on the bluebottle—careful with Ashok. Hold him! Hold him! Aunty! Bunty! Kanti! Oh, my gods! Ashok! You dropped him, you *mutha chodes*! Ashok. What's happened to you, my friend? Have you broken your patella? Oh, my gods. *Arrey bap re bap!* Manoj?! How will we manoj? Uncle! His ankle! I think he's broken his ankle, Uncle, and his patella. He can't shoot the rest of the film. My Bollywood classic has turned into a Greek tragedy! Uncle, call an ambulance. Tell them Ashok Patel has broken his patella! How can we ever replace you? Ashok. It's such a shock. Uncle. Aunty. Bunty. Kanti. Vaat ve'll do?

ANIL *sees* JOHN.

Oh, my gods. Is it my lucky day? Have the clouds parted and sent me a beige angel? Come here, Southern Star. *Aaja.* Come come.

DANNO *pushes* JOHN *forward.*

You, you showed me no manners before. But manners have no place in India. We are shooting a Bollywood blockbuster with the Ashok Patel …

DANNO: Pretty awesome, hey Johnny?

ANIL It's called *Bindhi Beach: Bollywood to Bondi!* I'm India's number one director. And you, *you* must replace Patel while Patel's patella gets a replacement. What is your good name?

JOHN: John Green.

ANIL: No, not your stage name. *Aapka asli naam.* Your real name?

JOHN: That is my real name.

ANIL: What sort of a name is that? Harshit! Teach him the curry-ography! Hardik! Make up his make-up. Kanti! Can't you hear me? Put some ice on Patel's patella!

JOHN: Thank you, but I'm not interested in your *Bhindi Beach* film.

DANNO: What?

ANIL: You're not?

Pause.

JOHN: No. I'm an Aussie.

ANIL: Do you know what you're giving up? Look at me. In my turd eye. You're turning down the opportunity to star in the most important movie made for the biggest film industry in the world?

JOHN: Sorry—it's just not me. It's not what I want. It's … not who I am.

ANIL: Tell me then, Mr Green … who are you?

SCENE SEVEN

BRONWYN *joins* JANELLE BURNS *shopping.* JANELLE *has a broad Australian accent.* HEATHER, *a sales assistant, enters. She has a sort of British accent and works as a receptionist.*

BRONWYN: How cute are these baby booties, Janelle? Should we buy them with the matching bib?

JANELLE: I prefer the clothes at the baby warehouse in Castle Hill.

BRONWYN: Trust me. City stores have better quality clothes. It's worth the RiverCat ride in. It's a lovely day out.

JANELLE: I wanna get that *Bee Gees for Babies* CD. Hmm. Mr Squiggle versus The Wiggles. Old school, new school or 'Play School'. Oh, I get so anxious every time I leave the Hills District.

BRONWYN: Janelle, let me buy them all for you. To celebrate your business award and our future grandchild.

> JANELLE *breaks down.*

Don't be upset, Janelle. It's a wonderful achievement that Burn Baby Burn's been nominated for an award. It's the best barbecue warehouse in Western Sydney. You'll win the award for sure.

JANELLE: It's not that, Mrs G. Of course I'm gonna win the award. It's just …

> JANELLE *sighs.*

BRONWYN: What's the matter, Janelle?

JANELLE: I don't know, I've just been totes emosh these last few weeks, Mrs G.

BRONWYN: You have? Have you been feeling sick too? In the morning?

JANELLE: No. Thank the Good Lord. I don't want a baby right now, Mrs G.

BRONWYN: Of course you do, Janelle.

JANELLE: Burn Baby Burn's my baby. I don't have time for an immaculate conception.

BRONWYN: You can run a business and have a child too, darling, look at Lisa Kenny!

JANELLE: You mean Lisa Curry-Kenny. She got married.

BRONWYN: Well, she'll always be Lisa Kenny to me.

JANELLE: But she was born a Curry.

Pause.

Mrs G, Johnny would freak out if he knew we were scouting different baby stores every week. I've stashed all of the accessories at the back of the warehouse. I hate keeping secrets.

BRONWYN: Me too.

JANELLE: Mum and Dad are putting pressure on me. Worse still, Chillsong are threatening to cancel my Gold Membership. I don't want to blow this up into biblical proportions, but it's just so wrong to be having sex out of wedlock.

BRONWYN: There's nothing wrong with it, Janelle.

JANELLE: There is. I'm on a highway to hell.

BRONWYN: Is John still insisting on wearing condoms?

JANELLE: Yes.

BRONWYN: Idiot.

JANELLE: That's it, Mrs G. No more condoms.

BRONWYN: Wonderful.

JANELLE: No, Mrs G. No more sex before marriage. I think this baby planning is messing with my morals. It's making me schizo. I love sex. I really do. I wanna have it all the time now, but I know it's wrong. I'm a sinner and a saint, Mrs G.

BRONWYN: Janelle, open your base *chakra*. Let your *kundalini* run free.

JANELLE: My Chillsong sisters are calling me Mary Magdelene.

BRONWYN: Marriage is overrated, honey. Olivia Newton-John's marriage to Matt Lattanzi failed and her second partner got lost at sea.

JANELLE: Mrs G, I just want a white wedding.

BRONWYN: Janelle, I just want a w— I just want a baby.

JANELLE: Sometimes I wish I lived in a country which was free enough to force us into an arranged marriage.

BRONWYN: What rot.

JANELLE: Look, Mrs G, I appreciate your coaching, but I'm gonna do this the traditional way. I'm gonna force John to marry me. I'll propose to him on the awards night. It'll be perfect. Then we can have a baby, not a bastard.

BRONWYN: Darling, let's be realistic. You and John have only been together for three years. Modern men take an average of six to eight years before they'll even think about proposing. Ring and dress shopping takes another year. Finding a venue, inviting the guests. It'll take another decade before you become a mum. Your eggs are on a timer, darling. If you don't turn them over easy, they could get scrambled.

JANELLE: But you had Livvy when you were forty-five.

BRONWYN: Ah yes, but not every woman has been blessed with a wondrous womb like mine.

HEATHER: Excuse me. Can I help you? Bronwyn, it *is* you!

BRONWYN: Janelle—to the RiverCat.

HEATHER: I haven't seen you for nearly thirty years! Heather Diaz. You look so different now.

BRONWYN: I'm sorry. I don't … know you.

HEATHER: It's me. Heather. My uncle sponsored you when you—

BRONWYN: I think we should go, Janelle.

JANELLE: What about the bibs and the booties and the Bee Gees?

HEATHER: Bronwyn. My daughter was the flower girl at your wedding.

BRONWYN: I didn't have a flower girl at my wedding.

HEATHER: How could you not remember? My husband gave you free counselling when you were depressed. I helped you paint over the graffiti at the front of your house the night after the Olivia concert. How could you forget that?

BRONWYN: I don't know what you're talking about.

HEATHER: I'll never forget that night … Do you still own that silver sweatband?

BRONWYN: I've never seen this woman before in my life.

HEATHER: It's me. Heather. We went to accent correction classes in the seventies.

> BRONWYN *and* JANELLE *start to exit.*

BRONWYN: Come on, Janelle. Let's go. We'll be late for the beautician. You must be curated for consummation.

HEATHER *exits.*

JANELLE: Okay. I'll try for a few more weeks. I'll prick holes in the condoms again, but if it doesn't work this time—you need to arrange the
marriage. Deal or no deal?

BRONWYN: Deal.

SCENE EIGHT

French photographer, GUILLAUME GUILLOTINE, *enters.* DANNO *and*
JOHN *enter.* JOHN *is dressed as Ginger Meggs in a red wig.*

GUILLAUME: *Bonjour, tout le monde. Bienvenue* to Waterloo. Today, I'm
proud to say we have hundreds of beautiful, sexy, *tête rouge flambée.*
So I need to split you like carrot tops *julienne. A gauche les Gingers,
à droit les rangas, et au centre … tout les Fanta Pants.*

He organises the audience.

JOHN: Do you think this guy will mind if I just take my Fanta pants off
and keep my shirt on?

DANNO: You're still embarrassed about your pepperoni tits, aren't ya?

JOHN: Shut up, Danno. Not everyone has perfect pink nipples like you
do.

DANNO: I'd prefer to have your big brown areolae any day.

JOHN: I still think you should have dressed as Annie.

DANNO: *You* should have dressed as Annie.

JOHN: I'm happier as Ginger Meggs.

DANNO: You know they made a black remake of *Annie.*

JOHN: What's that got to do with me?

DANNO: It's a great film.

JOHN: Blannie? Sounds ridiculous.

DANNO: It was an important cultural statement.

JOHN: I can't believe you asked that guy to wash the whiteface off.

DANNO: It's offensive.

JOHN: It was just a tribute to Ronald McDonald. Red-dy to red-gister?

DANNO: Stop making ginger jokes, man. Only redheads can make those
jokes.

GUILLAUME: *Okay, les fire-crotch, les ginger minges, les rusty crutches,
les strawberry blondes et les blueys …* your backsides will be the
backdrop. Bald butts to the back, and to the front, the hairier *derrières.*

SANDY enters, dressed as Ginger Spice in a British flag dress and wearing a red wig.

Ah oui, Ginger Spice, you come with me. You will be my *cause célèbre!* All the other tributes—Nicole Kidman, Ed Sheeran, Little Mermaid—to the front!

JOHN: Look, Princess Fiona from *Shrek* is wearing greenface! Is that wrong too?

DANNO: You're such a hypocrite. You'll celebrate Ginger Pride Day, but you refuse to come to Parramasala Festival with me … I created a once-in-a-lifetime opportunity for you, and you turned your back on Dixit.

JOHN: I'm just not into Dixit.

DANNO: You support Anglophilia, but reject any other culture. You're completely colour blind, but not in a healthy way. You're nothing more than a chromophobe!

JOHN: I am not a chromophobe.

DANNO: Worst of all, you dare to bludgeon Blannie!

JOHN: Blannie is a terrible concept. Annie is, was and always will be a redhead. By supporting Blannie, you're turning on your own kind. It's a bashable offence around here.

DANNO: You need to wake up.

JOHN: *You* need to wake up. You're happy to come to Ginger Pride, but when I suggested we go to Mardi Gras together—computer says, *'No!'*

DANNO: I've heard enough.

GUILLAUME: [*to* DANNO] Ron Howard, you come with me.

He moves DANNO to the other side of the stage.

Positions, s'il vous plaît … today's pose is juxtapose … *donc, allez,* do that.

He addresses the audience, pretending they're his rally crowd.

Mes petits Rougettes, ecoutez-moi! As you know, we applied to shoot everybody in Auburn but the council didn't permit more shooting in the Middle West. In a protest, you will show your *coq sportif*, your *coq au vin* and all your bits. Now you show your hide and hide no more. While I shed my *tri-couleur*, you show your true-colour … *Rouge!*

Today we end the Red-pression. Today begins the Red-volution. *Vive la Red-volution. Bouge la Rouge! Bouge la Rouge! Bouge la Rouge!*

> GUILLAUME *pushes* JOHN *and* SANDY *together, and exits.*

ALL: *Bouge la Rouge, Bouge la Rouge, Bouge la Rouge!*
SANDY: You?
JOHN: Well well well. Miss Heckler.
SANDY: You're that Cockney Convict from the Quay.
JOHN: Former … Cockney Convict. That was a past life.
SANDY: Cockney Convict to Ginger Meggs … nice career progress.
JOHN: Nice outfit.
SANDY: Today I'm Ginger Spice. Happy Ginger Pride!

> SANDY *throws what looks like red powder into the air.*

JOHN: What is it?
SANDY: Paprika. When I go to Mardi Gras I throw glitter everywhere, so I thought I'd throw paprika everywhere for Ginger Pride.
JOHN: I've never tried paprika.
SANDY: How can you not have tried paprika?
JOHN: I don't like spicy foods.
SANDY: That's ridiculous. Try some.

> *She puts her finger in the bag.*

Just dab it on your gums.

> JOHN *allows* SANDY *to put her finger in his mouth and try the paprika.*

JOHN: Cocaine flashbacks. Mmm. It's actually quite nice.
SANDY: Spice up your life.
JOHN: Never thought I'd see you wearing a Union Jack. Isn't that a little hypocritical?
SANDY: I'm about to tear it off … in protest.
JOHN: Great protest.
SANDY: Art has always been the best form of protest.
JOHN: What do you know about art?
SANDY: I'm a fan of Guillaume's work. I've always wanted to be in one of his photos.
JOHN: Glad to re-meet you.
SANDY: Glad I got you re-trenched.

JOHN: It was a blessing in disguise.

SANDY: Good. Happy Ginger Pride Day. I'm Sandy.

JOHN: John. Happy Valentine's Day. I'd still really like to take you out to say thank you.

SANDY: I'm really busy at the moment. I've gotta go to work straight after the photo shoot. We're launching on Saturday.

JOHN: How's it all going?

SANDY: Pretty frantic. I've gotta fly to Melbourne for a meeting in the morning and then fly back. City of Sydney are auditioning dancers and tour guides for my company.

JOHN: I've got a big day tomorrow too.

> GUILLAUME *re-enters.*

GUILLAUME: *Bouge la Rouge! Bouge la Rouge! Okay, tout le monde …* we're ready. Repeat after me: *Liberté, égalité, nudité!* I said, *'nudité'.*

JOHN: I'm feeling really itchy.

SANDY: Where?

JOHN: Can you scratch my—?

GUILLAUME: Stop talking during my photo shoot! [*To* JOHN] Art demands silence! You don't understand art. You want to stand out? You can go first, *agent provocateur!* Who are you supposed to be anyway, Prince Harry in a terrible *toupée*?

SANDY: He's Ginger Meggs.

GUILLAUME: Well, Megg yourself scarce, Scary Spice!

JOHN: She's Ginger Spice.

> GUILLAUME *pulls off their wigs.*

GUILLAUME: *Qui? Quoi? Qu'est-ce qui ce passe?* This is not your real hair! You are brown gingers!

SANDY: So what?

GUILLAUME: You look like jaffa cakes. *Je déteste choc-orange!* This rally is for real redheads only!

SANDY: Are gay marriage rallies only for gay people?

GUILLAUME: Today is the celebration of Ginger Pride. To show *'La Passion du Rouge'.* Now you must go.

JOHN: My face is itchy.

SANDY: Really?

JOHN: My throat feels swollen too.

SANDY: Oh, my God, your face has gone blotchy.

> JOHN *starts to panic.*

GUILLAUME: *Sors d'ici!*

JOHN: You paprika poisoned me!

SANDY: Stop being so dramatic. You just need an antihistamine.

JOHN: My whole body's itching!

SANDY: Should I take you to hospital?

GUILLAUME: *Dégagez-vous!*

SANDY: Is your skin okay?

JOHN: No. It's super sensitive right now. I think I've pumiced too hard.

GUILLAUME: *Cassez-vous!*

SANDY: [*to* GUILLAUME] We're not leaving.

GUILLAUME: *Depart!*

SANDY: No!

GUILLAUME: *Merde!*

SANDY: I never thought French people could be so arrogant. What a pig.

JOHN: I think I need to see a doctor.

SANDY: I'll drop you to RPA. Let me Judge Judy this guy first.

JOHN: [*to* SANDY] You're incredible, Sandy.

GUILLAUME: *Allez, quitter,* piss off!

SANDY: We're *not* leaving.

GUILLAUME: You go or I quit!

SANDY: We're not getting kicked out of a Ginger Pride rally for not being ginger!

GUILLAUME: Don't make me see more red than I already am! If you won't leave, I will. *Tout le monde.* We take the bus to La Perouse. The French never win at Waterloo.

> GUILLAUME *and* DANNO *exit.*

SCENE NINE

JOHN *enters with a chair. He sits.* MERLE *enters.*

MERLE: John Green?

JOHN: Yes.

MERLE: Step into my theatre.

JOHN: Theatre?

MERLE: My operating theatre.

JOHN: Doctor, why do I need an operation? It was just an allergic reaction.

MERLE: Boo!

JOHN: You? Oh, my God.

MERLE: What?

JOHN: Merle, you look strangely like my sister.

MERLE: I do?

JOHN: Yeah. It's an incredible resemblance.

MERLE: She must be a very beautiful girl.

JOHN: She's a brat most of the time. Mum asked me to pick her up from her piano teacher's house recently. The music teacher's didn't believe we were related, so she wouldn't let Livvy get in the car with me. Livvy thought it was funny and pretended I was a stranger. The teacher called the cops on me! No-one believes we're related because she's so fair.

MERLE: Little white lies.

JOHN: What are you doing at Prince Alfred Hospital?

MERLE: Tell me about your allergy? How long have you been hyper-sensitive?

JOHN: Since childhood.

MERLE: Yes. I had this allergy too.

JOHN: You did?

MERLE: I was born with it.

JOHN: You were?

MERLE: Yes. My childhood in … Tasmania. I was born there, you see. I hated it. I moved to France. I moved to London. I met the right people.

JOHN: I need to meet the right people too. I need to get this job on 'Bondi Parade' tomorrow. Have you started Humperdincking me yet?

MERLE: I have, but it may not be in the way you're expecting.

JOHN: I don't need any help with my family, I need help with my career. How did you become famous, Merle?

MERLE: By hiding the truth. My ambition may have taken me to Hollywood, but my deceit took me to the top. I worked with the best of the best. Sir Laurence Olivier. Good old Loz. I took my secret to my deathbed. Even my gravestone says that I was born in Tasmania. It wasn't until years later that it all came out.

JOHN: What came out?

MERLE: I'll tell you. In standard Merle time. I was trying to pass through to the other side but I got bailed up for faking my I.D. 'No devil's allowed up here. Even if they are Tasmanian,' they said. 'How on Earth can I get through? I said. 'On Earth, indeed. You claim you're Australian? Then it's high time you did something for your supposed homeland. The sunburnt country needs a new rebel, requires a new Gandhi! We received mail, ouija mail! Here's your chance to go back and correct your *karma*. Recruit the right person, help that candidate find their true identity, then you can move on!'

JOHN: I'm not your guy, Merle.

MERLE: I need to shave your head.

JOHN: What?

MERLE: You'll need a walking stick.

JOHN: Why?

MERLE: You'll have to wear glasses.

JOHN: I prefer contacts.

MERLE: Circular glasses.

JOHN: I'm so confused right now.

MERLE: So we'll wrap you in a *lungi*—

JOHN: What's a *lungi*?

MERLE: You must be abstinent and practise non-violence!

JOHN: This is a case of mistaken identity.

MERLE: It's you. It has to be you.

JOHN: I just wanna be on 'Bondi Parade'.

MERLE: But you're the Gandhi of Greystanes!

JOHN: *Go away!* Leave me alone!

> MERLE *goes to exit.*

Wait. Should I still see a doctor for my spice allergy?

MERLE: I'm your doctor now, John. And the operation has already begun.

SCENE TEN

JANELLE *enters with a barbecue on wheels.* JOHN *enters with* LIVVY.

JANELLE: Praise Jesus!

JOHN: What's the matter, Janelle? I'm late for my audition.

JANELLE: What took you so long? I need your help now. It's an emergency. Barbie's upset. *Aaaaarrrrrrggggghhh!* Barbie's burning!

JOHN *fixes the barbecue.*

JOHN: It's just the gas.

JANELLE: Notice anything different about me?

LIVVY: You're orange.

JANELLE: It's a spray tan from the Beauty Spot salon in the city. Don't you think I look healthy, wealthy and perky?

JOHN: You like a Cheezel.

JANELLE: Well, your face looks a bit red too. Are you hosting kids' parties again and not telling me?

JOHN: No, Janelle.

JANELLE: If I find Elmo or Darth Maul face paint anywhere, you're in trouble.

JOHN: What do you want, Janelle? I drove all the way back here to help you and I got fined for talking on the phone.

JANELLE: Well, get a headset. Like the one you wore to your 'X Factor' audition.

JOHN: I told you never to bring that up again.

JANELLE: You forgot about Valentine's Day yesterday.

JOHN: I thought you hated V Day?

JANELLE: I just say that.

JOHN: I've been busy with Cockney Convict Walking Tours. It was—is— an all-consuming job.

JANELLE: We never spend any time together. It's your day off and you didn't even wanna spend it with me.

JOHN: You're working.

JANELLE: Well, one of us has to work a proper job.

JOHN: I've gotta get to the audition.

JOHN *goes to leave.*

JANELLE: Wait. I didn't just call you here to fix Barbie. Dad just told me he wants to retire from Burn Baby Burn to take up a missionary position. He wants me to run the business … but not on my own. I need a right-hand man.

JOHN: Who else would … oh.

JANELLE: Quit acting. Quit that crappy convict crap. Burn Baby Burn's ours. It's bloody ours, baby. You'll have full-time job security. A steady income. Sick leave. Compo. I'm a sure thing to win the award this weekend. They'll brag about me in the local rags? I'll be famous in the *Daily 'Stanes*.

JOHN: I've gotta go.

JANELLE: John, listen to me. I need you all day Saturday. I need you at the pre-awards drinks. I need you to watch me get my make-up done. Then we'll get a limo to Greystanes RSL. Then I'll win the award. Then we'll bask in my glory at the after party. It's the most important day of my life, our lives and our afterlives. Promise you'll be there. This Saturday. Swear on my Bible app.

JOHN: I swear. Saturday I'm all yours.

LIVVY: Johnny, you're really late.

JANELLE: Livvy, can I have a moment with John. Alone?

LIVVY *leaves.*

JANELLE: I know you're in a rush, but let's have a quickie.

JOHN: I've got to go.

JANELLE: It'll only take a minute.

JOHN: Later.

JANELLE: Come on, babe.

JOHN: You're such a typical Gemini. One minute you're a nun, the next minute you're a nymph. I'm going to my audition.

JANELLE: Australia only worships sport, John. You know that. You should have kept playing footy. You were so good at it. You would've been a star by now. On TV. Regardless of whether you're black or white or English Irish Dutch French Portuguese or whatever your mum says you are. It doesn't matter with footy … But acting? Mel Gibson can play a Scotsman. Russell Crowe can play an Italian gladiator—

JOHN: Janelle, can you stop?

JANELLE: Nicole Kidman can play a French prozzy.

JOHN: I don't wanna talk about this!

JANELLE: Cate Blanket played the Queen Of England.

JOHN: Blanchett.

JANELLE: Meryl Streep played Lindy Chamberlain.

JOHN: Yeah. And they flew in a dingo from Singapore Zoo to star in that telemovie.

JANELLE: All dingoes are Aussie, John.

JOHN: Nah, just the blonde ones. They had to import a black one. They're the only ones that steal.

JANELLE: That's not funny, John.

JOHN: Yes, it is.

JANELLE: I'm worried about you, babe. About the future. What characters will you be able to play if you keep trying to be an actor? Taxi drivers?

JOHN: Is that how you see me?

JANELLE: No, babe. I see you as my partner. Burn Baby Burn's the best barbecue warehouse in Western Sydney. It'll be ours. But you've gotta show me how committed you are. We need to make a formal commitment to each other 'cause I can't live like this anymore. You've gotta make a choice. It's me … or your acting.

SCENE ELEVEN

We hear the theme song to 'Bondi Parade'. JANELLE *transforms into the* 'Bondi Parade' RECEPTIONIST. *She answers a phone.* JOHN *and* LIVVY *enter.*

RECEPTIONIST: 'Bondi Parade' casting. Tricia speaking. Yes, we've received the Logie Award invitations. We'll get back to you shortly. 'Bye.

JOHN: Good afternoon. I'm John Green. I'm here for the—

RECEPTIONIST: Oh, thanks for coming at short notice.

JOHN: Umm, that's okay.

RECEPTIONIST: Where are the other three cleaners?

JOHN: I'm not a cleaner. I'm here for the audition. Here's my headshot. I've got a sporty one, a suited one, this one's with stubble and in this one I'm wearing fake glasses. Oh, and this is my goofy comic one—I've got my mouth wide open—see?

RECEPTIONIST: Casting's finished. You're two hours late.

JOHN: What?

LIVVY: Just let him in.

RECEPTIONIST: Soz. No can do.

JOHN: I've been looking forward to this audition. I've been preparing for this role my whole life.

RECEPTIONIST: The producers have left.

JOHN: I played a skull called Yorick in Bankstown Drama Society's *Halal Hamlet*. I played a statue in *Pygmalion* … the reviewer said I was deeply 'moving'.

RECEPTIONIST: It's just an extra role.

LIVVY: His drama teacher said he was extra-ordinary.

RECEPTIONIST: Then you're over-qualified.

LIVVY: Then what's the problem, lady?

RECEPTIONIST: You're just not the look they're going for.

LIVVY: What do you mean he's not the right look?

RECEPTIONIST: I'm not saying 'right', they just took a different direction.

JOHN: I'm great with direction … even if they're different.

RECEPTIONIST: *Go away!*

JOHN: I played Camper Number Two in *Away*.

RECEPTIONIST: I'll call the police.

JOHN: Please don't. I've pumiced myself for weeks now.

RECEPTIONIST: I beg your pardon?

LIVVY: John, let's go.

JOHN: Please let me stay. Just let me sit in the green room.

RECEPTIONIST: Look, if you're that desperate for some work, apparently City of Sydney are holding auditions across the road for something or other. You might be better suited for that.

> *The* RECEPTIONIST *leaves.*

JOHN: City of Sydney?

> *Pause.*

Livvy. I'm gonna pretend to be Aboriginal.

LIVVY: What?

JOHN: If anyone asks, I'm Aboriginal.

LIVVY: You not allowed to say that word.

JOHN: It's an Aboriginal dance company. I met the artistic director. I'm gonna audition.

LIVVY: You can't say Aboriginal anymore, Johnny. They told us at school.

JOHN: I'm gonna pretend to be Indigenous, then.

LIVVY: Better. But still not cool.

JOHN: Livvy, I'm deadly!

LIVVY: John, this is unethical.

JOHN: Ethics. Ethnics. Same diff.

LIVVY: Indigenous Australians aren't ethnic.

JOHN: I know. It's just a joke, Livvy. Chill out. It's so hard to be PC these days.

LIVVY: You've lost the plot. We're going home.

JOHN: No, we're not. We're goin' bush.

> JOHN *and* LIVVY *exit.*

SCENE TWELVE

The City of Sydney PRODUCER *enters.*

PRODUCER: Thank you, John. That was an interesting interpretative dance.

JOHN: Glad you liked it, brudda. So are there only white fellas on this board? Where's Sandy?

PRODUCER: Sandy sent you? Oh, good. She's caught up in Melbourne where they're holding auditions for the Victorian troupe.

JOHN: Right on, sista. That's deadly.

PRODUCER: Deadly indeed. Well, we loved your audition. The job's yours.

JOHN: Really?

PRODUCER: Yes, we love Sandy. She's got a great eye for talent. Rehearsals start tomorrow. First tour launches this Saturday.

JOHN: Saturday?

PRODUCER: Yes. It says on your application that you're available to start work straight away. You didn't lie on your application?

JOHN: Ah—no. I'm available Saturday.

PRODUCER: Good. John, you left the origin box blank on your application. Which—ah—mob are you from?

JOHN: Mob?

PRODUCER: Where are you from?

JOHN: Ah … I'm from … from … Northern Territory. Arnhem Land.

PRODUCER: You're a Yolngu boy?

JOHN: Yep. True Yolngu boy.

PRODUCER: So you speak Yolngu too?

JOHN: Fluently.

PRODUCER: Wonderful. Which island?

JOHN: Crocodile Island.

PRODUCER: Near Gananggarngur Island?

JOHN: Yep.

PRODUCER: I adore the Crocodile Island group.

JOHN: [*sung*] 'My island home'.

SCENE THIRTEEN

BRONWYN, JOHN, JANELLE *and* LIVVY *gather around the barbecue, drinking cask wine.* LIVVY *'s screeching budgies can be heard inside.*

BRONWYN: A toast to Janelle and her awards on Saturday. To Janelle!

ALL: To Janelle.

BRONWYN: [*whispered to* JANELLE] Don't worry, Janelle. The sting will go away.

JANELLE: Good.

BRONWYN: [*whispered to* JANELLE] I put some horny goat weed in John's Vegemite.

JOHN: What are you two whispering about?

JANELLE: Nothing.

JOHN: Do you have any fake tan I can borrow, Janelle?

BRONWYN: What?

JANELLE: I've got bucket-loads. Now have you made your decision about you-know-what, John?

The bird noises grow louder.

BRONWYN: Oh, Livvy, is it really that hard to breed a yellow willie wagtail budgie?

LIVVY: A yellow-faced violet recessive pied spangle budgie, Mum. And yes. It's very hard.

JANELLE: Poor Dicky can't get hard.

JOHN: Janelle. Don't blaspheme.

JANELLE: Whoops. Blasphemy bag.

LIVVY: Why won't Dicky do Fanny?

BRONWYN: Yes. Why won't Fanny get pregnant?

JANELLE: Give him time, Livvy. Debbie didn't do Dallas in a day. [*To* JOHN] Now what's your decision about Burn Baby Burn?

JOHN: Well … I've thought about it a lot and … Oh, man. I'm losing it. I've lost it already.

JANELLE: What, the ring?

JOHN: No, my job. I got fired.

BRONWYN: What?

JANELLE: That's perfect.

JOHN: Not fired. Retrenched. I … Janelle … I … I've quit acting. Let's run Burn Baby Burn together.

JANELLE: Oh, my God. Really?

LIVVY: John!

JANELLE: You're gonna quit acting and work for—work with me? Really?

JOHN: Yes.

JANELLE: Oh, my God! Blasphemy bag.

LIVVY: [*whispered*] I thought you were going to tell her that you wanna work for Sandy instead.

JOHN: [*whispered*] I wanted to but I couldn't.

LIVVY: [*whispered*] You like Sandy, don't you?

JOHN: [*whispered*] Livvy, shhhh.

LIVVY: [*whispered*] The awards are on at the same time as Sandy's opening.

JOHN: [*whispered*] I know.

LIVVY: [*whispered*] You're in a real pickle, bro.

JOHN: [*whispered*] I hate pickle.

JANELLE: What are you two whispering about?

JOHN: Nothing.

JANELLE: John, focus. This is gonna be so good for business. I'll … we'll be the pride of Greystanes.

BRONWYN: Livvy, to bed. Janelle, take John upstairs and *celebrate* together. I'm going to go and put on some relaxing music.

> BRONWYN *exits.*

LIVVY: Why John?

> LIVVY *exits.*

JANELLE: I thought they'd never leave. I had an Italian boyfriend once, his family were glued to him. Wog families. Hahaha. Sometimes it's so hard to be alone with you, Johnny.

JOHN: We're not a wog family, Janelle.

JANELLE: I know.

JOHN: You shouldn't use that word. It's racist.

JANELLE: You've changed your tune, Mr Singaporean Dingo.

JOHN: Words are powerful. They have a frequency.

JANELLE: I know. I'm not racist. I'm religionist. When are you gonna start coming to Chillsong with me? It's so lovely. Particularly the chapel.

JOHN: The theatre is my church, Janelle.

JANELLE: Not anymore. Babe … I can't hold this in any longer. I've gotta tell you something about your mum. I hate keeping secrets from you, but I've got to be honest. She's gone too far. We've been going baby clothes shopping together. Every week. She really wants for us to settle down. She wants grandkids real bad. Do you?

JOHN: Want grandkids? Um, shouldn't we have kids first?

JANELLE: Exactly.

JOHN: There's plenty of time for that. We need to build our Barbie Empire before we start buying Barbie Dolls.

JANELLE: I agree. But your mum's trying to force us to have kids.

JOHN: I know. I saw her Genetic Spawn.

JANELLE: You are her genetic spawn. What's that awful noise?

JOHN: Oh, my God.

JANELLE: Don't blaspheme. What's up?

JOHN: Mum's *not* playing Olivia Newton-John music.

JANELLE: What's she playing?

JOHN: I think it's Billy Idol.

JANELLE: What song?

JOHN: 'White Wedding'.

SCENE FOURTEEN

JOHN *does a really bad version of an Indigenous dance.* SANDY *enters and sees him dancing.*

SANDY: What the hell was that?

JOHN: The choreographer taught it to me.

SANDY: What are you doing here?

JOHN: You hired me.

SANDY: No, I didn't.

JOHN: Well, it's not my fault you were in Melbourne. Your white fella funding club at City of Sydney loved me.

SANDY: You're unbelievable.

JOHN: I'm a scallywag. I know.

SANDY: You can't work in this company.

JOHN: I already am. I've got a lot of experience in tour guiding. I know all the facts.

SANDY: Facts? You have a lot to learn about facts.

JOHN: Well, I'll learn it. Teach me.

SANDY: I wouldn't know where to start.

JOHN: Did you enjoy the show today?

He starts doing his dance again. SANDY *laughs.*

How did the auditions go in Melbourne?

SANDY: More 'authentic' than the Sydney ones.

JOHN: Why are you always picking on me? I had to go to hospital because of you.

SANDY: I can't help it if you got spiced out! You can't be in the troupe.

JOHN: I love that word. Troupe. Bring in the troupes …

SANDY: Mate, this is serious.

JOHN: I love your company logo, Sandy. Did you design it yourself?

SANDY: I did.

JOHN: It's really clever.

SANDY: Thanks.

JOHN: I've never felt part of a team before. Not even with footy. I love being in your troupe. I really like wearing your company shirt.

SANDY: Hate being an Indian giver, but you gotta hand it back.

JOHN: Even Gav let me keep my convict outfit as a souvenir.

JOHN *takes the company shirt off, revealing a hypercolour t-shirt.*

SANDY: You're wearing a lot of layers for summer.

JOHN: I don't wanna get burnt.

SANDY: Yuck, the shirt's all sweaty.

JOHN: What can I say? I'm hot.

SANDY *laughs.*

SANDY: Hypercolour?

JOHN: Yep.

SANDY: I used to love hypercolour.

JOHN: I still love it. I've got hypercolour socks and even briefs. This is the only hypercolour shirt I have that still changes colour, though.

SANDY: It seriously still works?

JOHN: Yep. Give me your hand.

SANDY *gives him her hand. He puts it on his heart. The shirt changes colour where* SANDY*'s hand was—leaving a handprint on his heart.*

Please don't fire me, Sandy. I couldn't handle being fired twice in the same month.

SANDY: I don't want to fire you but I have to.

JOHN: I can't be a convict, I can't be a beach extra, I can't be in your dance troupe. I've been pumicing my skin for months now. All over my body. Now I'm fake-tanning myself so I can be in your company. I'm losing my mind. I don't know where the hell I fit in anymore. I'm between a rock and a blackface.

Pause.

SANDY: Okay. You've got a month to find another job and then you're out. I'll try and find a place for you in the troupe. But I'm taking you out of the dance sections and you can only do the narrations.

JOHN: Thank you, Sandy.

SANDY: You're putting me in a really compromising position.

JOHN: Awesome.

SANDY: I don't know why I'm doing this. I'm gonna get in so much trouble if anyone finds out.

JOHN: No-one will find out. Everything'll turn out alright.

SANDY: I highly doubt it.

JOHN: You dare doubt the hypercolour briefs man?

SANDY *laughs.*

SANDY: Have you really been sanding yourself?

JOHN: No. Yes, I'm even sandier than you.

SANDY: That isn't funny. It's concerning.

JOHN: I know. It's not so easy to change colour, unless you're hypercolour.

SANDY: You wanna learn some things about us fellas?

JOHN: Yes.

SANDY: Lunch. My shout. I'll debrief you.

SCENE FIFTEEN

BRONWYN *and* LIVVY *wait nervously.* JANELLE *enters, holding a trophy.* JOHN *enters sheepishly.*

JANELLE: You've got real nerve showing up now.

JOHN: I'm sorry, Janelle. My new boss—I should have told you, I got another tour guide job.

JANELLE: You're a liar. You said you quit. You're so selfish. You've ruined my night. You've ruined my life.

JOHN: I'm so sorry.

JANELLE: You had no intention of ever running Burn Baby Burn with me, did you?

JOHN: I did. But then I got offered this other tour guiding job. It was unexpected.

JANELLE: You're a liar! I never want to see you again.

LIVVY: Thank God.

JOHN: Janelle—

JANELLE: I don't want to be in your screwed-up family. Get out of my sight.

> JOHN *begins to walk away.*

BRONWYN: Keep calm, Janelle.

JANELLE: Shut up, Mrs G! Don't you walk away from me, John Green!

> JOHN *continues to walk away.*

Bastard! Everyone knows that you're the milkman's son!

BRONWYN: There was no milkman!

JANELLE: How else could he be black and his family be white? Look at your little sister. She's white and you're black.

BRONWYN: He's not black.

JOHN: I'm not black. Livvy's cheap shoes are black. My hair is black. I am not black.

LIVVY: You know what will be black though? Your eye.

BRONWYN: We are British!

JANELLE: Who was that Heather lady?

BRONWYN: Our ancestors are Anglo-Saxon Normans. Anglos from Denmark. Saxons from Germany. Normans from France. You know, British! Like all other British.

JANELLE: What about the graffiti?

BRONWYN: With a little Swedish Viking thrown in. Your grandmother's village was pillaged when they built the first Ikea store in Leicester.

JOHN: So you're saying Grandpa was a Leicester molester?

BRONWYN: Yes, but Swedish. Your grandmother's hair was red like rubies and her skin was as white as the cliffs of Dover. She was the quintessential English rose!

JANELLE: What a load of shit.

LIVVY: So Gran was a granga?

JOHN: Are you even my mum, Mum?

BRONWYN: Of course I'm your mother, darling. There's no milkman. I swear on God. I swear on Olivia Newton-John!

JANELLE: I never want to see your family again. The wedding is off!

JOHN: What wedding?

JANELLE: She bleached my fanny!

JOHN: What?

JANELLE: Your mum's an absolute psycho. Not only did she force me to go to the intimate bleaching salon, she bought me Pink Pecker cream so I'd bleach your pecker pinker!

JOHN: Mum!

JANELLE: And she pressured me to use Pink Wink cream to whitewash my vertical smile!

JOHN: Mum, is this true?

BRONWYN: No!

JOHN: Pink Pecker cream?

BRONWYN: Janelle's lying.

JANELLE: I'm not! She thinks that if my lady bits are pinker, that she'll get grandchildren.

BRONWYN: I've never heard of Pink Wink cream!

JANELLE: She bought a super pump pack! You and your family are insane! You're dumped, John.

BRONWYN: No! Dashed are my dreams of being a grand-MILF!

JANELLE: I would never want a child that could inherit your genes! I'm not your lab rat anymore!

JOHN: Janelle—

JANELLE: She groomed me to become a monogamous nymphomaniac! I'm a good Christian girl!

BRONWYN: You're a fake and a phony and I wish I'd never laid eyes on you!

END OF ACT ONE

SCENE ONE

JOHN *stands onstage debating whether to wear his green contact lenses.*
MERLE *enters, frantic.*

MERLE: My gravestone! My grave!

JOHN: Not now, lady ghost.

MERLE: Don't you call me a ghost! Once I had a fulsome figure, but now, I'm entirely apparitional.

JOHN: I'm pretending to be entirely Aboriginal.

MERLE: I know. The pretending has to stop! My whole life was an extended lie and all I have left is a grave of deceit. My gravestone is cursed!

> *Pause.*

I'm … I'm not Tasmanian. I just wanted to get in with Flynn. But he was more interested in his 'merry men'. If I told the truth, I never would have reached the heights that I did.

JOHN: I understand.

MERLE: I know you do. We're mutually entwined. I may be flawed and fractured, but I'm still your spirit guide.

JOHN: My mum's messed up and I reckon only you can help her.

MERLE: She's quite something.

JOHN: Help her to help me? Please?

MERLE: Mahatma's mother needs help too? That wasn't part of the plan.

JOHN: Please, Merle. If you fix her then I'll be whoever you need me to be. Deal or no deal?

MERLE: I shall dig to the depths of your mother's secret chamber. Deal.

SCENE TWO

ANIL *enters.* JOHN *enters wearing a hoodie and sunglasses.*

ANIL: [*to an optometrist offstage*] Doctor? Where's my order? Fifteen parcels of the blue. Another fifteen of the grey/blue lenses. Fifteen of the violet blue lenses and twelve parcels of the aquamarine. *Jaldi karo*, mate. I haven't got all day.

JOHN: Indian actors wear coloured contact lenses?

ANIL: Of course, my new cast are arriving from India today. How else can I make them look natural and sexy. Who are you—the Grim Reaper?

JOHN: Shhh. I don't want my new girlfriend to bust me here. I'm trying to wean myself off contacts.

ANIL: Then why are you at the optometrist?

JOHN: I'm lapsing.

ANIL: Hey—I remember you from *Bindhi Beach* when Patel's patella was broken. I never forget a face. Good, bad or ugly.

JOHN: How did *Bindhi Beach* turn out?

ANIL: Let's just say it's lucky you didn't replace Patel.

JOHN: Why?

ANIL: The production was cancelled. My Indian money-man thinks this country is dumb, drunk and racist.

JOHN: Wasn't that a TV show?

ANIL: That's why he got that impression. So he pulled the plug on the finance.

JOHN: Sorry to hear that. Do you think we are?

ANIL: Personally I don't see it. But that might be my cheap contacts. Either way, I'm getting a lot of work here. More than I ever did in Bombay.

JOHN: I thought you were huge over there?

ANIL: No, that was Daddy Dixit—Anil the Second. He won nine FilmFare awards in a single year. My granddaddy Anil Dixit the First, founded the FilmFare awards, which explains why he won so many.

JOHN: So why didn't you get the same treatment?

ANIL: Somebody changed the bloody rules. Nepotism has a use-by date. My first masterpiece, *Gondwanaland*, was ripped to pieces by the press like the tattered tectonic plates of a jigsaw puzzle.

JOHN: Is that why you came here to do *Bindhi Beach*?

ANIL: Ya, I thought I could make it here, and show those buggers back home who's boss. But the script was such a cliché. Kangaroos, koalas … How often do you see those animals at Bondi Beach? Then Patel broke his patella. I thought fate is not on our side. But then I saw you, and destiny smacked me in the face. We Indians know when we sense destiny. But you turned your back on it.

JOHN: Destiny?

ANIL: Australia gave me a second chance. I would like to give you one too. I'll be shooting a self-funded Bollywood musical.

JOHN: You're shooting here?

ANIL: We couldn't shoot in Calcutta because many of the old British buildings are falling apart. In Sydney your historic buildings are new. So we'll recreate Calcutta in Sydney. Won't be too hard, scrape off some paint, a few cracks in the facades, open up the sewers, faint waft of cedar wood and urine, unfinished monuments. We already have permission to shoot in the Queen Victoria Building, by the Queen herself.

JOHN: Really, the Queen?

ANIL: Yes, Clover Moore. The film is called *Addy*. It's set in eighteen seventy-eight in Calcutta and is based on a true story. It's about the first Indian actor who played Othello in India, Baishnab Charan Addy. For many years in colonial India only white British actors were allowed to play Othello. And they wore blackface. Addy was the first native Indian man to play Othello without blackface. The casting of Addy inspired Indians to stand up to their colonial masters and win their country back. So it's a very important film. You see?

JOHN: Not quite. So it's a film about the first brown man to play a black man on stage in white colonial India?

ANIL: Precisely. [*To the optometrist*] *Eh jaldi karo*, mate. Where are my contacts?

JOHN: Anil, don't make a spectacle.

ANIL: Okay I'll keep calm and cut to the chase. Do you have an agent?

JOHN: I do, but she's always tied up.

ANIL: Never mind, I want to be your agent. Give her the bird, now you work with Anil Dixit the Third. *Theek hai?*

JOHN: What?

ANIL: You don't speak Hindi?

JOHN: No. Why would I?

ANIL: I'll teach you. It means 'okay'.

JOHN: Ah tick ay. Anil, don't you want me to audition?

ANIL: No, auditions are futile. It is your destiny to play Addy.

JOHN: Can I think about it? I need to run it by my girlfriend Sandy.

ANIL: We're having a huge press conference in a few weeks and I want for us to perform a few live scenes and a big dance number at the event. Just to get the international press talking.

JOHN: Where's the press conference?

ANIL: I've hired the most amazing space in Sydney.

JOHN: The old amphitheatre at Australia's Wonderland?

ANIL: No. The studios where they film 'Bondi Parade'.

SCENE THREE

Circular Quay. SANDY *and* JOHN *enter.*

SANDY: Part with the pumice.

JOHN: I have. I pumice I have.

SANDY: Do you feel bad about Gav?

JOHN: Do *you*?

SANDY: It was time for him to retire. I didn't think they'd shut him down so soon, but at least we've got our turf back.

JOHN: He got what was coming to him, I guess.

SANDY: Yeah.

> *Pause.*

When can I come hang out in Greystanes?

JOHN: When the track work finishes.

SANDY: When's that?

JOHN: Never.

SANDY: Why not?

JOHN: State Rail.

SANDY: Say no more. Grey stains … what a funny name for a suburb. It reminds me of dirty laundry. How come you haven't invited me over to yours yet?

> *Pause.*

Tell me about your folks? Where are they from?

JOHN: My parents are British. From Leicester. Leicester molesters.

> SANDY *raises an eyebrow.*

Tell me about your parents?

SANDY: Mum's a dealer.

JOHN: What?

SANDY: Art dealer. She spends a lot of her time travelling. She's a Wiradjuri woman. She's involved in a research and restoration program with elders in the community.

JOHN: Did the language die out?

SANDY: A lot of it. But it's coming back.

JOHN: Good. I think Livvy did an assignment on you … guys after a school excursion to Wagga Wagga.

SANDY: You can say mob—it's okay.

JOHN: Nah. It's not for me to—

SANDY: Just say it.

JOHN: Sandy—

SANDY: Mob.

JOHN: Mob.

SANDY: We all need a mob.

> *Pause.*

Tell me about your dad.

JOHN: He died when Livvy was born. Heart attack. Mum won't let us talk about him. What about yours?

SANDY: Dad's a professor of Indigenous art and culture.

JOHN: Wow. Your parents sound amazing.

SANDY: Is John Green your real name?

JOHN: Everyone always asks that. Yeah, it is. I was named after John Travolta. My sis was named after Olivia Newton-John. My mum's obsessed with Olivia. Hey, your parents didn't name you after Sandy from *Grease*, did they?

SANDY: Are you kidding? How tacky. No. I was actually named after the Sandy Desert.

JOHN: Awesome.

SANDY: When my parents first got together they drove across the desert.

JOHN: You're named after your parents' first holiday. That's so sweet.

SANDY: My parents are awesome. You'd love them. Dad's Maori. He's from Whakapapa [*pronounced 'Fhakapapa'*].

JOHN: Where's that?

SANDY: New Zealand. North Island.

JOHN: That's fantastic [*said with a very bad New Zealand accent*].

> *Pause.*

SANDY: Have you been looking for a new job, babe? It's been a month.

JOHN: I've landed one, babe.

SANDY: Where?

JOHN: I've been cast in a film that's being shot here.

SANDY: That's amazing!

JOHN: It's about the first Indian man in Calcutta to play Othello on stage—without blackface.

SANDY: Couldn't Indians play Othello before that?

JOHN: No. It's set during the British rule. White men up until then played Othello with blackface.

SANDY: Makes me mad just thinking about it.

JOHN: I love it when you get mad.

SANDY: Sounds like an important film. It's pretty amazing that Indians were able to get their turf back from the British. Great role for you.

JOHN: I'm not sure if I'm right for the role.

SANDY: Why wouldn't you be?

JOHN: Well, I … I'm not … Maybe it is the right vehicle for me. I don't know. I'm terrified. The director wants to do a live preview of one of the dance numbers at a press conference in a few weeks.

SANDY: So you're doing a staged version of a film about an actor who's in a play about Othello.

JOHN: Yes. Something like that.

SANDY: I bet your mum'll be happy if you get this film.

JOHN: She's never happy with me.

SANDY: I spoke to my dad today. He invited you over for lunch this weekend.

JOHN: Really? Don't you think it's a bit too soon to be meeting your dad?

SANDY: It's not a formal thing. It'll be just like hanging out with mates. Dad's really cool.

Pause.

JOHN: I'm not ready.

SANDY: It'd mean a lot to me.

JOHN *is nervous.*

JOHN: I can't. I'm just not ready.

SANDY: I really want you to meet my family.

JOHN: So do I. When I'm back on track.

SANDY: Why won't you meet my dad?

JOHN: My family don't even like me, why should yours?

SANDY: He's super cool. You'll love him. I'll sort out lunch for this weekend. Mum wants to meet you too, when she's back from New York.

JOHN: I said no. One mum's too much for me. I can't handle two.

SCENE FOUR

A Skype ringtone is heard. BRONWYN *enters, searching for her mobile. She answers it.*

BRONWYN: Who would be calling me on Skype? [*To the phone*] Hello? I don't really know how to work this app on my phone.

    MERLE *enters, also on Skype.*

MERLE: Hello, is this Bronwyn Green?

BRONWYN: Yes. Speaking. I can't see you very well. The image is very dark.

MERLE: Ha. Bronwyn, this is Olivia Newton-John.

BRONWYN: What?

MERLE: This is Olivia Newton-John. I thought I'd call you to thank you for all of your posts on my fanpage.

BRONWYN: Oh, my God. Olivia? Is it really you?

MERLE: Yes. I love interacting with my fans and I thought I should reach out to you.

BRONWYN: Olivia. I … I'm …

    She bursts into tears.

I'm so happy to hear from you. You're my guiding light.

MERLE: Well, I'm trying to be.

BRONWYN: I'm your biggest fan, Olivia.

MERLE: I know. I know. You told me in one of your posts that you were looking for a wife for your son? Well, my daughter's recently single, so I thought we could introduce them to each other? It's high time I became a grand-MILF.

BRONWYN: Oh, Olivia, I feel the same way! Yes! Let's marry them off. John will change his last name! I'll change mine too!

MERLE: I'm actually in Greystanes at the moment and I thought we could go and grab a bite to eat?

BRONWYN: I … I don't know what to say. Of course!

MERLE: I've kept your address from all of your fan mail from the eighties. I'm actually at your front door.

The doorbell rings. BRONWYN *freezes.* MERLE *enters in shadow.*

BRONWYN: Olivia?

MERLE: Yes, Bronwyn?

BRONWYN: I can't see you properly. The lighting is very dim.

MERLE: We need an Obie light.

BRONWYN: A what?

MERLE: Never mind. Bronwyn, if our children get married, I'd be happy for my daughter to change *her* last name to Green.

BRONWYN: Newton-John is the perfect last name, though.

MERLE: My daughter's last name is Lattanzi, though.

BRONWYN: Of course it is. How could I forget?

MERLE: Lattanzi is an Italian name.

BRONWYN: I thought your first husband was American?

MERLE: His family are Italian and they're not from up north.

BRONWYN: Oh.

MERLE: If we become grand-MILFs together our grandkids will be very, very *dark*.

The lights snap to bright. BRONWYN *sees* MERLE *and screams.*

BRONWYN: You're not Olivia!

MERLE: No, I'm not.

BRONWYN: Get out of my house!

MERLE: John told me you were a piece of work, but I didn't expect this.

BRONWYN You know John? Are you from Fertile Fallopians?

MERLE: Wrong. My business is not with John anymore.

BRONWYN: It isn't?

MERLE: No. You're the one that I want.

SCENE FIVE

LIVVY *enters and walks to her birdcage. The birds are very quiet. She looks into the breeding box. The life-size budgies do an interpretative egg-laying dance.*

LIVVY: It's a miracle! Fanny's laid an egg! Dicky's done the deed. They got physical! My birds have laid! We've got eggs! I'm so eggstatic!

JOHN *enters.*

JOHN: That's fantastic, Livvy! Your budgies finally bonked.

LIVVY: What's bonked?

BRONWYN *enters, tampering with her phone.*

JOHN: Doesn't matter. I've got some good news too. Mum, can you listen to me for a second?

BRONWYN: Hang on. I just need to block this stalker.

JOHN *looks at his mother's phone.*

JOHN: Mum—that's my picture! What are you doing?

BRONWYN: It's just this new app I've discovered. Fertile Fallopians. It shows you all the frisky women in the vicinity.

LIVVY: Are you a lesbian, Mum?

BRONWYN: No, darling. I'm pretending to be him.

JOHN: Mum!

BRONWYN: Look, darling. There's Barbara, Betty, Bianca, Briony. And that's just the B's. What's best is that you can refine the search within five kilometres so they'd at least all be members of Greystanes RSL. You never need sign your members in ever again.

JOHN: Christ, Mum. You've even filed them into alphabetical order!

BRONWYN: So many wonderful wombs in close proximity.

LIVVY: You know in some countries matchmaking is a celebrated part of society.

JOHN: Delete the app. Now.

BRONWYN: I can't. It's pokies for the promiscuous. I only just got a straight flush.

JOHN: You're an addict. Gimme the phone.

BRONWYN: No, I'm on fire!

JOHN: Why is my pic filtered?

BRONWYN: I had to filter it. I'm better at being you, than you.

JOHN: Delete it now.

BRONWYN *reluctantly deletes the app.*

I've gotta tell you something important.

BRONWYN: What on earth is it?

JOHN: I've been cast in a movie. As the lead.

BRONWYN: Congratulations, darling! Your first film!

BRONWYN *hugs* JOHN.

JOHN: It's just a little arty film.

LIVVY *hugs* JOHN *as well.*

LIVVY: My brother's a star! C'mon, budgies, leave the shell! Now, I just want my British budgie eggs to Breggsit.

LIVVY *heads to the attic.*

BRONWYN: Where are you going? I thought we were going to watch the 'Grease Singalong Rockin' Rydell' edition.

LIVVY: I thought you wanted me to clean out the attic?

BRONWYN: Clean the attic. Then we'll rock the Rydell edition.

LIVVY *exits the room.*

So, Johnny. Who's the director?

JOHN: He's … he's from … Indi … Indianapolis. Midwestern American guy.

BRONWYN: How wonderfully cultural, darling!

JOHN: Mum. I've got something else I need to tell you.

BRONWYN: Oh.

JOHN: I've met a girl.

BRONWYN: Oh, thank God.

JOHN: I really like her. It's all moving really fast. I've decided to meet her dad. I want you to meet her soon.

BRONWYN: Wonderful. What's her name?

JOHN: Sandy.

BRONWYN *is filled with joy once more. We hear the chorus of 'You're the One that I Want' from* Grease. *An* OLIVIA LOOK-ALIKE *struts onstage and dances around* BRONWYN. *She's pregnant.* BRONWYN *is over the moon.*

SCENE SIX

Sandy's dad, MANA, *enters doing a fierce traditional Maori welcome dance to* JOHN *called 'Powhiri'.* SANDY *watches.* JOHN *is nervous.* MANA *ends suddenly. He has a Maori accent.*

MANA: *Nau mai ki toku fare.* Relax, bro. I just welcomed you to our home.

JOHN: Thank you. Quite a welcome.

MANA: You look like you shat yourself. Next time do it in the garden, the plants could do with some fertiliser.

JOHN: It's a nice garden.

MANA: Nah, it's full of crap from all of Sandy's exes who also shat themselves after my *Powhiri* welcome dance.

JOHN: Interesting water feature. What is it—the Elephant Man?

MANA: Nah, son, it's Ganesh.

JOHN: Ganesh the garden gnome?

MANA: No, Ganesh the Indian elephant god. The remover of obstacles. Don't you know him?

JOHN: No.

MANA: Can't blame you. He's one of a billion. Takes more than a lifetime to learn 'em all. Probably why they invented reincarnation.

JOHN: How do you know about that stuff?

MANA: Each year in India they hold a huge festival of Ganesh, called Chaturthi.

SANDY: Dad went there last year to see it.

MANA: It's fascinating. Thousands of Hindus carry giant elephant statues to the beach where they submerge them in the ocean for blessings and purification. Last year there was one at Dandi Beach in Gujarat, the very same beach where Gandhi finished his salt revolt.

JOHN: Sounds like an assault on the senses.

MANA: Indigenous cultures all over the world use water to purify.

JOHN: I often swim in Bondi Beach.

MANA: Me too. When I grew up in Whakapapa [*pronounced 'Fhakapapa'*], there was nowhere to swim. Just a ski field.

JOHN: 'Whakapapa'. What does that mean?

MANA: Ancestry. Makes sense, ay? Whoever your papa fucked, that's your ancestors.

>   *Beat.*

So, John, I heard you pretended to be a black fella to get a job in Sandy's dance company.

JOHN: I did.

MANA: Back in the eighties, Sandy's mum pretended to be Indian to get work.

JOHN: Really?

MANA: Yeah. When we first met, it was tough to get our careers started. It was just something that we had to do to make ends meet. While I was writing research papers, Katrina had to go out and get a normal job.

SANDY: Mum loved the ritual of getting ready for work. Every morning she'd stand in front of the mirror and wrap herself in a *sari* to prepare for the day. The final touch was always the red *tika*.

JOHN: What's a *tika*?

SANDY: It's the red dot that married women wear on their forehead. For two years Mum pretended to be an Indian woman. She couldn't get close to anyone at work 'cause she didn't want her identity to be revealed.

MANA: Can you believe, back in the eighties a local grocery store wouldn't give a job to an Aussie black girl, but they would to a newly arrived 'fake' immigrant?

SANDY: I loved watching Mum wear the *sari*. It's so elegant and feminine. Dad liked it too.

MANA: Yeah, but I preferred when she wore nothing at all.

SANDY: Dad!

MANA: She'll be back from New York soon. You'll get to meet her, John. She'll be thrilled to meet our new honorary black fella.

JOHN: You don't need to call me that. It's all good.

MANA: Why not? I thought you wanted to be a black fella.

JOHN: I don't like the word black actually. I think it's derogatory.

MANA: What do you mean, boy?

JOHN: Well, the history of the word has negative connotations. Words are important. This tablecloth is black. Your jeans are black. My jacket is black. I am not black. I used to get called 'blackie' all the time when I was a kid and I hated it.

MANA: You've got to turn that around. You've got to own it. Don't let other people water you down. It doesn't matter what your background is. Whether it's Maori, Mayan, Middle East or Middle Earth. You can still be an Aussie. Nobody dictates identity, just you. Rise above it. Be proud. Be yourself.

Pause.

You've never been with a black girl, have you, John?

SANDY: Dad—

JOHN: No.

MANA: I can tell. I better go check the jerk chicken, it needs more spice.

MANA leaves. JOHN is slightly awkward.

JOHN: Hope I didn't upset him?

SANDY: No, he likes you.

JOHN: I think he called me a jerk.

SANDY: He was referring to the chicken.

JOHN: Sometimes I get a little worked up.

SANDY: Don't worry. My family loves a good argument.

JOHN reaches into his pocket and pulls out an envelope.

JOHN: Here's my resignation letter.

SANDY: Thank you. I know it meant a lot to you.

JOHN: I'm grateful that you've allowed me to be in your company.

SANDY: If it were up to me I'd love you to stay. It's just not fair. On the others.

JOHN: I know. It's not fair.

Pause.

SANDY: When can I meet your mum?

JOHN: Soon. Give me time.

SANDY: You haven't been wearing your green contact lenses.

JOHN: No.

SANDY: I think you look much more handsome without them.

JOHN smiles. He holds SANDY's hand.

JOHN: I like the look of my hand up against yours. And my arm. And my body.

SANDY: It was weird for you, wasn't it?

JOHN: What?

SANDY: When we first got naked together. I could see you were freaking out over your skin up against my black skin.

JOHN: You're not black.

SANDY: Hey. I'm black.

SCENE SEVEN

On one side of the stage, the several eggs that FANNY laid, hatch. Humans, dressed as baby birds wearing budgie smugglers, emerge. FANNY and

DICKY *dance with their baby budgies.* JOHN *and* SANDY *enter and the birds stop the dance. We are at the* Addy *launch.*

SANDY: Wow. I didn't think the press would get the blackface dance sequence—but they loved it. So wrong, yet so poignant. How do you feel now about starring in an Indian film?

JOHN: I tore down my 'Bondi Parade' posters. It felt weird. I couldn't bring myself to throw away the framed cast poster though.

SANDY: I'm so excited about meeting your family. Where are they?

JOHN: Ah …

SANDY: My dad's here. He can't wait to meet your mum.

> JOHN *is suddenly angry.*

JOHN: Sandy, I specifically told you.

SANDY: He wanted to see a snippet of the film. Don't worry. He loved it.

JOHN: I'm not ready for our parents to meet yet.

> BRONWYN *enters.*

BRONWYN: Darling. Where's the American director from Indianapolis?

> ANIL *enters, and a moment later a caucasian woman,* RENEE, *enters.*

ANIL: [*seeing her*] Renee! I found our Southern star. [*To* JOHN] John, this is none other than the Executive Producer of 'Bondi Parade'! Renee Brogan, meet John Green.

> RENEE *shakes* JOHN'*s hand.* JOHN *is incredibly excited.*

RENEE: That was a wonderful performance, John.

JOHN: Thank you. I'm so honoured.

RENEE: Listen, We're having to urgently recast a new role. I think you'd be perfect.

ANIL: Lead role, Johnny boy. They're looking for a tall, dark, handsome actor to play the new doctor on the Parade.

BRONWYN: He's definitely tall and handsome.

ANIL: John, I've bent over backwards to get you this audition.

RENEE: Anil's been very accommodating with his dates.

ANIL: The character has his own surgery on 'Bondi Parade'. Renee's promised me the shoot would be over in a few weeks and that it wouldn't clash with *Addy*'s dates. Great publicity for *Addy* too. All I have to do is teach her more *tantra*.

RENEE: Shoosh. [*To* JOHN] The audition's tomorrow. I've hand-delivered the script to Anil. Rush home and learn those lines because the audition's tomorrow. I have to run. So I'll see you in the morning, John?

JOHN: Absolutely.

ANIL: I've got to go and talk to the press. Renee, *tantra* tonight.

RENEE: Sure, but don't touch.

ANIL: That's the point.

> RENEE *and* ANIL *exit.*

SCENE EIGHT

SANDY *is waiting to meet* BRONWYN. JOHN *realises that it is time to introduce them. He gathers all of his courage.* LIVVY *is also present.*

JOHN: Ah … Mum, I … I want you to meet … Sandy, you should meet my mum. Sandy, this is my mum Bronwyn. Mum, this is … Sandy.

> BRONWYN *stares at* SANDY. *She was expecting something different and is awkwardly silent.*

SANDY: It's so lovely to meet you, Bronwyn.

BRONWYN: It's Mrs Green.

SANDY: Oh, sorry. You look amazing, Mrs Green.

> MANA *enters.*

Dad, come and meet John's mum Bronwyn.

BRONWYN: It's Mrs Green.

MANA: *Kiaora*, Bronwyn. Give us a *hongi*!

> MANA *rubs noses with* BRONWYN, *then sticks his tongue out. She screams. Suddenly* JANELLE *enters in a huff and walks up to* JOHN.

JANELLE: John. I'm preggers.

BRONWYN: What?!

MANA: You cheating on my daughter?

JOHN: Absolutely not. Janelle, what are you talking about?

JANELLE: I read in the newspapers that you were going to be here. I had to tell you. I'm so proud of you, babe.

SANDY: What's going on?

BRONWYN: No condoms are going on! Finally!

MANA: I knew you were a jerk! I should teach you a real lesson, about manners.

MANA *grabs* JOHN. SANDY *stops him.*

SANDY: Dad, please, just calm down. Remember your vow of non-violence.

JANELLE: I'm sorry for what I said about the milkman, Mrs G.

LIVVY: Come on, Janelle. Let's get some fresh air.

JANELLE: But—

LIVVY: You look flushed.

BRONWYN: Janelle, I can't believe it.

JANELLE: Oh! It just kicked! I feel a pain in my womb, Mrs G!

LIVVY: Let's go.

LIVVY *leads* JANELLE *offstage as* SANDY *re-enters.*

SANDY: Is that your ex?

BRONWYN: Ex? It's his girlfriend.

JOHN: Mum! That's not true.

SANDY: Why would your mum lie?

BRONWYN: Exactly.

JOHN: Mum, this is Sandy's dad Mana.

BRONWYN: Don't touch me!

MANA: It's an exchange of breath, a sharing of souls.

BRONWYN: My soul needs saving. SOS!

JOHN: Mum—

BRONWYN: Let's go.

JOHN: Don't be so rude.

BRONWYN: This is 'Bondi Parade'. This is what you've always wanted.

SANDY: John—

JOHN: Sorry, Sandy—I have to go.

SANDY: What?

JOHN: I'll call you tomorrow. I have to nail this audition.

BRONWYN *begins to lead* JOHN *out of the room.*

SANDY: Nice to meet you, Bronwyn.

BRONWYN *looks back at* SANDY.

BRONWYN: It's Mrs Green. Livvy, c'mon we're going!

JOHN *pulls away from* BRONWYN.

JOHN: Wait for me in the car, Mum.

SANDY: Dad, could you wait outside for me please?

BRONWYN: Come on, John. It's late, it's getting too dark.

MANA: At our darkest moments we need the most enlightenment.

MANA *exits*. BRONWYN *exits*.

JOHN: I'm so sorry, Sandy.

SANDY: I can't believe you ignored my dad.

JOHN: I'm scared. I've never moved so fast before.

SANDY: You've been cheating on me with your ex.

JOHN: I'm not cheating on you. I swear.

SANDY: Worse than cheating is ignoring my family. Nobody ignores my family.

JOHN: I didn't mean to ignore your dad. You shouldn't have brought him without telling me, that's all.

SANDY: He wanted to support you. God, how many restrictions can one relationship have? I'm not allowed to ask where you're from, my dad can't come to your launch, I can't meet your family.

JOHN: I'm sorry my mum's awful. Do you want to come over to Greystanes?

SANDY: She won't want me there.

JOHN: I want you there.

SANDY: You've got to learn your lines for 'Bondi Parade'.

JOHN: I wanna be with you.

SANDY: This is what you've always wanted, John. Isn't it?

JOHN: Yes.

SANDY: Have you been sleeping with your ex? Tell me the truth.

JOHN: Not since I met you. I promise. Please, babe, will you come back to mine tonight?

SANDY: Don't call me babe. Your ex is pregnant. This isn't gonna work. I don't believe you. I don't trust you. Everything about you and your family seems to be based on lies and secrets. It's just not me. It's over. I'm done. I never wanna see you again.

JOHN: Sandy—

SANDY: I'm out of here.

JOHN: Sandy, please.

SANDY: I never wanna see you again. It's over.

SCENE NINE

At the 'Bondi Parade' studios.

JOHN: Stand back. Give her some breathing space or we'll lose her. Hurry up, we need a bandage to stop the bleeding, someone take their shirt off. Hang on, I'll do it myself. How long was she under water for? Lucky I'm a doctor. Tomm-o call an ambo, Dav-o was she at the bottle-o? She's blowing point oh-seven. I can smell it on her breath. Dean-o alert the chopper, mate, looks like we'll need to do a sea-vac. I'm gonna have to give her mouth-to-mouth … Oh, Kimbo. It's you. What are you doing here? Haven't seen you since school. I heard you fell off a cliff last year? Good to see you bounced back.

RENEE: That was wonderful. I'm pretty certain all the female viewers will want mouth-to-mouth from you. Now can we just try that with an Indian accent?

JOHN: I beg your pardon?

RENEE: Could you do the monologue again, but with an Indian accent?

JOHN: When the regular cast auditioned, did you ask them to perform with an English or Scottish or Irish accent?

RENEE: No. But that's different.

JOHN: Why is it different?

RENEE: I'll ask you again. Could you do the monologue with an Indian accent?

> JOHN *takes some time debating whether he should do it or not.*

JOHN: My best redhead friend Danno had skin cancer. He's always wished he was brown. He used to sunbake as often as he could. And then he got sick. We were in and out of every hospital in Sydney and I got to know all of the best doctors. Dr Shah, Dr Singh. Dr Chen. Dr Nguyen. Dr Tran. Dr Chandrabalan. All born in Australia. All with Australian accents. If you want 'Bondi Parade' to be the realistic show that it claims to be then—

RENEE: Hot bronzed bodies that live at Bondi Beach. That's the realism, buddy. Now just do it with the accent.

JOHN: I'm sorry. I don't think it's appropriate.

RENEE: I don't see what the big deal is. Indian accents are funny. Anil makes me laugh. He's so witty. Can't you try to sound like him?

JOHN: Anil's accent is authentic to him. He was born there.

RENEE: Our plot lines have been heavy lately since the bluebottles stung Beryl and the fish and chip shop ran out of vinegar and poor Beryl had to pee on herself. Point being, we need our storylines to be lighter. We need funny Dr Mistry! Our big brown mystery man. Now please do it with in the accent.

JOHN: I don't think you're seeing this from my perspective.

RENEE: Well, you don't see it from mine. I'm just working up brownie points with our overseas investors. We make most of our profit from selling the show overseas. The UK and American networks have threatened to pull out unless we put more diverse faces on TV. Apparently, 'diversity' is the new buzz word, and we're in the business of creating buzz. You'll be the best known brown doctor on Aussie TV. Dr Kumar Mistry. Have you got a sense of Kumar or not?

JOHN: I do have a sense of … Kumar. I just don't think it's me. I'm not your mystery man.

RENEE: That's a shame. Because I really would like to you to play Dr Mistry.

JOHN: You're actually offering me the role?

RENEE: Yes.

> *The theme song from 'Bondi Parade' plays.*

JOHN: I'd love to be in 'Bondi Parade', I just can't play this role. Can't Dr Mistry have an Aussie accent like everyone else?

RENEE: No.

JOHN: Then I don't want be on your show. I don't want to be on 'Bondi Parade'.

RENEE: You're turning down a role in the longest-running TV show in Australian television history?

JOHN: Yes, I am.

RENEE: Who the hell do you think you are?

JOHN: Isn't there another role I can play?

RENEE: Well, next season we'll need a disabled actor. Maybe you can do that?

JOHN: You're unbelievable.

RENEE: You want an acting career? … Break a leg.

SCENE TEN

JOHN, BRONWYN *and* LIVVY *enter.*

BRONWYN: Is Janelle really pregnant?

JOHN: It's a lie.

LIVVY: She does look a bit porky.

JOHN: She's lying.

LIVVY: She spewed outside of the studio.

BRONWYN: Morning sickness?

JOHN: At night?

LIVVY: She's lying, Johnny. She still loves you. And she just wants a beige baby as an accessory.

JOHN: Mum, Sandy broke up with me. I want you to call her and apologise to her.

BRONWYN: I'm not apologising to anyone. Go to Janelle! She's pregnant!

LIVVY: I thought you hated Janelle now.

BRONWYN: Should we do a DNA test?

JOHN: Yes. We should. On you, Mum.

> *Pause.*

BRONWYN: I'm cooking dinner tonight. To celebrate your audition. How did it go?

LIVVY: Why don't we invite Sandy around for dinner?

BRONWYN: And what would I cook? Braised bunyip?

LIVVY: Ming-Wa's mum cooked the most amazing Thai curry the other night. Everything you cook is bland, Mum. Can't you add coriander or chilli or something?

BRONWYN: Don't you say the C word again under my roof or I'll have to wash your mouth out. I hate chilli. It burns. How was the audition?

JOHN: Don't change the subject.

BRONWYN: I'm not. I just want what's best for you. Now tell me how it went.

JOHN: I've never been more humiliated in my life.

BRONWYN: What happened?

JOHN: She kept trying to force me to do it in an Indian accent.

BRONWYN: How awful.

JOHN: They offered it to me, but I said no.

BRONWYN: You've changed since you've been with this girl.

JOHN: For the better.

LIVVY: I think so too.

JOHN: Sandy's amazing. She's beautiful, she's smart. I've never met anyone so comfortable in their own skin. She runs her own company. She owns her own apartment in the city.

BRONWYN: So what? I'm the best careers advisor Greystanes High School has ever had.

LIVVY: Call her. Apologise. Stalk her. Beseech her. Besiege her if you must. Just like Dicky did Fanny.

> LIVVY *exits.*

JOHN: Sandy's better than any girl I've ever met. I love her.

BRONWYN: She's clearly been badly brought up.

JOHN: She's been brought up brilliantly.

BRONWYN: She called me by my first name.

JOHN: You seriously expect another grown woman to call you Missus?

BRONWYN: She's just not right for you. She's scattered.

JOHN: I'm the scattered one.

BRONWYN: Even if I did my reiki on her it wouldn't work. She has an extra layer on her skin. Too much melanin. It's scientifically proven to block UV and all the *chakras*.

JOHN: You attack everything that moves! What are you? A 'great white … *chakra*'?

BRONWYN: I just … Look, a mother knows these things. I've got nothing against her. She's just not your type.

JOHN: Say it. Just say it.

BRONWYN: If you have children together—how will they turn out? Hmm? Why don't you find yourself a nice Australian girl?

JOHN: Are you that stupid? How can you be a teacher when you're so fucking narrow-minded?

BRONWYN: Don't you ever speak to me like that. I feel a pain in my womb!

JOHN: She's more Australian than anyone could be! Sandy is the perfect Australian.

BRONWYN: Olivia is the perfect Australian. You should marry her daughter. And change your last name. John Newton-John. That has a lovely ring to it.

JOHN: Olivia's born in England, Mum. That makes her English. Just like you.

> LIVVY *enters frantically with her budgie cage.* FANNY *is attacking her babies. She starts pecking them violently. She attacks* DICKY *too. Blood squirts everywhere.* LIVVY *is screaming and crying.*

LIVVY: Fanny's gone crazy!

> *There is blood all over the cage and feathers everywhere.* FANNY *is tweeting loudly and madly. She is covered in blood.*

Fanny went crazy and pecked Dicky and my babies to death.

> DICKY *is in pieces and baby bird limbs are scattered.* FANNY *is screeching louder and louder. Many feathers fall from the ceiling, covering the whole stage.*

Do something, Johnny!

JOHN: Fill a bucket up with water. Quickly.

> BRONWYN *gets a bucket filled with water and gives it to* JOHN. LIVVY *is still hysterical.* BRONWYN *tries to calm her.* FANNY *is getting madder.* JOHN *grabs* FANNY. FANNY *pecks at him hard. Blood spills all over* JOHN*'s white shirt. He dunks* FANNY *into the bucket and drowns her.*

LIVVY: You're drowning her.

JOHN: I don't know what else to do. Dad used to do this if one of his budgies went crazy.

> FANNY *dies.* LIVVY *runs away crying.*

BRONWYN: Livvy!

> JOHN, *exhausted, observes the blood stain on his shirt from the birds. He has blood on his hands also.* BRONWYN *goes to him and begins to wipe the blood off his hands on to hers.*

Think of the future. Be smart. Don't be cruel.

SCENE ELEVEN

JOHN *is walking towards the ocean, holding his life-sized framed poster of the 'Bondi Parade' cast.* MERLE *is with him.*

MERLE: I know this is a big deal for you. You can do it. And then once you're done we could have a meal together at the Dahl Mahal in Harris Park? I'd ask your mother, but I fear she might attack me again with her garland of garlic. I'm not a bloody vampire, I'm an apparition. She even attempted to exorcise me by playing the theme song to *Ghostbusters*.

JOHN *looks at his poster and begins to cry.*

Salty tears. Count yourself lucky, the British would have taxed you for that. Are you really the next mahatma? The great soul. I remember reading about Mohandas Gandhi in the papers. It was 1930. I couldn't believe that only one man could be so defiant against the world's largest empire. The British had passed the Salt Act which prohibited natives to collect and sell it from the sea. They were forced to buy it from the British and pay hefty taxes. Gandhi's salt revolt lasted for three weeks, and by the time they reached the Arabian Sea, tens of thousands had joined them. It was the first large-scale non-violent civil disobedience movement. They ignored the act and collected salt from the sea. As did millions of other citizens around the country. I was in England and only nineteen. I was so torn between the two worlds, I half-cast myself in the murky English Channel, and decided to release my past. Then adopting my new role as a decent Tasmanian dame, I stiffened my upper lip, hitched down my petticoat, and bought a pound of non-taxed salted beef!

JOHN *immerses the poster into the ocean at Bondi Beach. They watch it float away.*

I'm proud of you, John. Unlike mine, your tears are now tax-free.

SCENE TWELVE

JOHN *and* DANNO *enter.*

JOHN: Thank you so much, Danno. You saved my arse.
DANNO: Any time. We promised that we'd bail each other out if either of us ever went to jail.
JOHN: I didn't know who else to call.
DANNO: I'm glad you did.
JOHN: Your house looks so … tidy.

DANNO: I can afford nice things now. I got a new job.

JOHN: What job?

DANNO: Don't worry, I didn't go back to SBS. I know you think sub-titles suck.

JOHN: I've actually been watching lots of foreign films lately.

DANNO: John … I have something to tell you.

JOHN: Let's just watch the State of Origin, Danno.

DANNO: I'm going for Queensland tonight. Does that piss you off?

JOHN: It doesn't bother me what side you're on, mate.

> *Pause.*

DANNO: I can't believe you got arrested for littering.

JOHN: I thought about throwing it in the dumpster, but I wanted to im-merse it in water.

DANNO: You could've sold it on eBay.

JOHN: It was more of a rite of passage.

DANNO: I can't believe I missed your passage.

> JANELLE *enters.*

JANELLE: Danno, why's your phone switched off?

> *She sees* JOHN.

Oh. What are you doing here?

JOHN: What are *you* doing here?

JANELLE: You didn't tell him yet, did you, Danno? I was gonna post our news on the 'Barbie Bulletin' first.

> *Pause.*

JOHN: No. No no. Is this a joke, Janelle? Danno?

DANNO: I … I—

JANELLE: We're in love. Danno loves me.

JOHN: What? How? When? What?

DANNO: We bonded while bitching about you.

JANELLE: He's the new co-owner of Burn Baby Burn. You're not the only one who's moved on, John Green. Danno was the perfect person to fill your gap.

DANNO: Figuratively speaking.

JOHN: I thought you wanted to go to film school, Danno.

JANELLE: Not anymore.

JOHN: Is it true about the baby?

DANNO: What baby?

JANELLE: Shhhhh!

JOHN: She said that she's pregnant with my baby.

JANELLE: No, I didn't! It's your baby, Danno.

DANNO: That's impossible. We haven't had sex yet.

JANELLE: We might have if you could get it up.

DANNO: I'm being respectful of you because you wanna wait till marriage.

JANELLE: I'm just saying that in case Jesus is listening. I need regular sex, Danno.

DANNO: What about your hymen restoration program? You told me it was as important to you as Jesus rising from the cave.

JANELLE: To hell with the hymen restoration program!

DANNO: Are you really pregnant, Janelle?

JANELLE: No. I made it up.

DANNO: Why?

JANELLE: To win him back.

DANNO: What about me?

JANELLE: I wanted him to be jealous. I still love you, John.

JOHN: If you loved me, you wouldn't have forced me to abandon my dreams.

DANNO: So you don't love me, Janelle?

JANELLE: Of course not.

DANNO: You're a piece of work, Janelle.

JANELLE: Oh, come on, Danno. Cut the crap. We all know that you're less interested in my barbecue and more interested in sausage.

DANNO: That's a lie. John and I came back here to watch the State of Origin. I love footy!

JANELLE: Of course you do—two dozen grown men groaning and groping at each other's tackle. You only shacked up with me to make John jealous too.

JOHN: You two deserve each other.

JANELLE: Danno, you're fired!

DANNO: Good, 'cause I'm burnt out. John, I'm sorry.

JOHN: Sorry I screamed at you at Ginger Pride.

DANNO: I've only ever wanted to help you with your career, Johnny.

JOHN: I know. Thank you for introducing me to Anil.

DANNO: It's a great fate, mate.

JOHN: Bring it in, brother.

>*They hug.*

I'm sorry I disappointed you, Janelle.

JANELLE: I only ever wanted to give you stability.

JOHN: I know.

JANELLE: I'm leaving Chillsong.

JOHN: Why?

JANELLE: I was only going 'cause my parents want me to. I have nothing against the church. I just don't like their bloody songs. I'm using my blasphemy bag money to join a surf goddess retreat in Byron Bay. I wanna be a happy hippy, not a cranky skippy.

JOHN: Good for you, Janelle—

JANELLE: Go to Sandy, John. You have my blessing.

DANNO: Go! Go and stop her at the airport.

JOHN: She's not at the airport.

DANNO: Oh.

JANELLE: Make like a boomerang and get her back. Go!

>JOHN *exits.*

DANNO: Janelle?

JANELLE: What, Danno?

DANNO: You're—

JANELLE: Dumped/

DANNO: Dumped.

JANELLE: I said it first.

DANNO: No. I did.

JANELLE: Fine. You still owe me one more shift.

DANNO: Really?

JANELLE: You, me, Oxford Street, Midnight Shift.

SCENE THIRTEEN

>SANDY *enters.* JOHN *follows.*

JOHN: Why haven't you returned my phone calls?

SANDY: I don't wanna see you.

JOHN: Janelle was lying. I promise.

SANDY: So many lies.

JOHN: These last few weeks have been awful without you. I miss you. I love you.

SANDY: Please leave.

JOHN: They offered me the role on 'Bondi Parade'.

SANDY: Good for you.

JOHN: I turned it down.

SANDY: Why?

JOHN: It's not what I want.

SANDY: What do you want?

JOHN: You. I know I'm a mess, but I'm getting my life together. The *Addy* shoot has been amazing. Why don't you come on set and watch the finale?

SANDY: I'm busy.

JOHN: I'm loving my costume. It's called a *kurta*. Wanna see some photos of me in it?

SANDY: No.

> JOHN *shows her some pics on his phone.*

JOHN: Please take me back, Sandy. Please.

SANDY: John. Please go. You have so much shit you need to sort out.

JOHN: I know.

SANDY: Shoot your film. Sort your shit out with your mum. I can't be the one to pull you out of this mess. Only you can.

JOHN: I need you.

SANDY: Give me some time, John. I need some time. Maybe we can meet in a few months. After your shoot. Okay?

JOHN: Will you have dinner with me tonight?

SANDY: No.

JOHN: My shout.

SANDY: Goodbye, John.

JOHN: Please? I'll cook you a curry.

SCENE FOURTEEN

JOHN *and* LIVVY *enter.* LIVVY *reveals an old piece of paper to* JOHN.

JOHN: What's this?

LIVVY: I found it in the attic when I cleaned it out.

JOHN *reads the piece of paper.*

JOHN: Why didn't you tell me?

LIVVY: I didn't wanna upset you. Have you looked in Mum's bathroom cabinet before?

JOHN: Only to borrow her toenail clippers. Why?

LIVVY: She has a secret compartment. With unlimited tubes of this.

LIVVY *hands* JOHN *a tube of Lighten Up skin bleach.*

JOHN: Lube? Oh. Lighten Up Lotion?

LIVVY: It's skin bleach, John. Do you think she bleached my skin when I was a baby?

JOHN: I don't know.

LIVVY *starts to cry.* JOHN *hugs her.* BRONWYN *enters.*

BRONWYN: Awww. How sweet. You were always good at pacifying her, Johnny. Do you know that when you were a baby, Livvy, John was nursing you once and you started sucking on his nipple. You thought it was mine. [*She laughs.*] I've always thought your areolas were abnormally large, Johnny.

JOHN: Mum.

LIVVY: I found this in the attic.

LIVVY *holds up the piece of paper.* BRONWYN *freezes for a long while.*

BRONWYN: It's just a prop I made up years ago for a school play I directed.

JOHN: Don't lie, Mum.

BRONWYN: I'm not lying. It's from a silly school play. One of my students made it as a joke.

LIVVY: Stop lying to us!

She holds up the Lighten Up tube.

Did you bleach my skin when I was a baby?

BRONWYN: No, darling! You were always naturally fair.

LIVVY: Really?

JOHN: Was I adopted from Fiji, Mum?

BRONWYN: No, darling! You're my very own. You came from this womb. Why are you being like this?

JOHN: This is your real birth certificate, isn't it?

BRONWYN: I told you it's a prop.

LIVVY: *Lies!*

BRONWYN: *Don't you raise your voice at me!*

> *Pause.*

LIVVY: I hate you!

BRONWYN: Such rude children! You've both ruined my life! I can't sleep anymore, I'm having horrific nightmares, I'm hallucinating, I hear voices in my head! I'm using a garland of garlic as numchuckers!

JOHN: Play on, Oberon. Play on.

BRONWYN: What did I do to deserve this?

LIVVY: What did I do to deserve my birds to die!

JOHN: We could go and buy some new budgies?

LIVVY: It's nearly impossible to breed yellow-faced recessive pied violet spangles. But I did it. It took me forever to get the right budgies so I could breed that specific colour.

> *She looks at her mother angrily.*

I'm going to Ming Wa's place.

> LIVVY *goes to leave.* BRONWYN *grabs her.*

BRONWYN: Make sure you put on your sunscreen. And lock the door behind you. Something is rotten in the state of Greystanes.

> *She grabs some sunscreen and applies it generously to* LIVVY's *face and arms.*

LIVVY: [*to* BRONWYN] I know it was you.

BRONWYN: What are you talking about?

LIVVY: You poisoned Fanny, didn't you?

BRONWYN: No.

LIVVY: Her shit was green before she went mad.

BRONWYN: Watch your mouth, young lady.

LIVVY: You fed her wheatgrass, didn't you? Or rat poison!

BRONWYN: I only gave her a slither of kale.

LIVVY: You poisoned the nest!

> BRONWYN *slaps* LIVVY.

SCENE FIFTEEN

ANIL *enters. We are on the* Addy *film set in Sydney.*

ANIL: Darren, Warren, Graham, good positions, perfect. Where are the two Toms? Tom … Tom, you got lost again? Satnav, Navman, next time show them the way. Okay, Britishers, red coats on. Muskets ready. Pump your muskets. Pump, pump, pump. But hold your fire. Don't shoot yet. Okay, put your pith helmets on. Deepak, why are there no pith helmets? Who keeps taking their pith? Bengalis, mount your tigers. Get ready to roar. Sharma! *Yeh kyaa hai?* Where are the snakes, Sharma? King brown, red-bellied black—the snakes in this basket are all Aussies. Sharma, I said non-venomous, fetch some snakes that don't bite. Elephants. Why do we only have ten? We need eleven elephants in this scene. Kanti, can't you count? Give it to Ganesh, this tusk is too hard for you? Now, lower the cow. Be careful not to puncture it. We can't use it if it's holey.

Pause.

Manoj, someone's missing. Where's my brown angel? Go fetch him from the trailer. Hey, Johnny my boy. Your Othello suicide dance will be a huge hit in India and inspire all the youth-in-Asia. Britishers, you will take the higher ground. So elevate your performance. Bengalis, you take the high *moral* ground. So levitate, levitate. But do it in sequence. Tit for tat. Elevate, levitate, elevate, levitate. Elevate, levitate. *Acha?* Pistols ready. Pyros ready. Dynamite ready. Okay, roll 'em. Go, John, start dancing. Yes. Yes. Yes. Step ball change. Slide to the right. So graceful. You're like a Hindu Fred Astaire. Pirouette. Double pirouette. Perfect canon. No, don't touch the canon. Hold fire everyone. John, don't come near the canon. Hold your fire …

Pause. Sound effect.

Oh, my gods! What just happened? *Oh, my gods!* His face is on fire. He's burning! His beautiful face is alight! It's like the Michael Jackson Pepsi ad all over again. Who shot their load on John's beautiful face!

We hear an ambulance siren.

SCENE SIXTEEN

We hear a hospital monitor beeping. JOHN *is wheeled on in a hospital bed, unconscious. His face is covered with bandages.* BRONWYN *enters. She holds his hand.*

BRONWYN: My beautiful boy. I owe you an apology. And an explanation.

    SANDY *enters, holding a bunch of flowers.*

SANDY: I'm so sorry, Mrs G. These are for you.

    Pause.

BRONWYN: Thank you, Sandy.

    SANDY *holds* JOHN*'s hand.*

SANDY: What's the prognosis, Mrs G? Will he recover?

BRONWYN: The doctor says he has fifty-fifty chance of being disfigured. It was so bad, the doctor thought he might need skin grafting, but thankfully once the swelling went down, we realised that only the first layer of facial skin had been burnt. When the scabs fall off, the doctor will decide what to do next. I trust Dr Sharma, we're in good hands.

SANDY: So we just wait?

BRONWYN: Yes. I've only had one hour sleep. I'm a mess. I've been praying all night. I don't know if I should use my rosary or Buddhist beads or crystals.

    MERLE *enters.* BRONWYN *sees her.*

I can't think clearly. I'm hallucinating.

MERLE: Do you believe in demons and *karma*?

BRONWYN: I do.

MERLE: *Chakras, karma, kundalini*—you know where they come from, right?

BRONWYN: I study the Western variation. John took me to rock'n'roll yoga in Bondi once.

MERLE: You're like my other half, Bronwyn.

SANDY: Do you pray, Mrs G?

BRONWYN: I chant. Only when my yoga app reminds me to. Do you?

SANDY: I do.

BRONWYN: Who do you pray to?

SANDY: To the earth. To the sky. To my ancestors. In Wiradjuri, we call our ancestors *balumbambal*. We speak to spirits. *Dhulubang*.

MERLE: Bronwyn, we're two of a kind.

BRONWYN: Who are you?

MERLE: I'm Merle Oberon.

BRONWYN: The Hollywood actress?

MERLE: Yes. You're an actress too it seems.

SANDY: I've been seeing spirits all of my life. My mum says it's a gift from our *balumbambal*. Don't you ever feel their presence? Their guidance?

BRONWYN: I talk to my crystals, but I'm not related to them.

MERLE: I was in a terrible car accident at the peak of my fame. I had scars all over my face. They created the Obie light, named after me to hide my scars. Camera technicians still call it the Obie light. You don't have a crew around you to conceal every detail, Bronwyn. You don't have a Hollywood husband like me to fabricate your past.

SANDY: Tell me more about your mother, Mrs G.

BRONWYN: Please, Sandy, call me Bronwyn. My mother was a mean woman. She used to tease me about my frizzy black hair. Her hair was auburn when the sun would shine through it. Beautiful.

SANDY: You'd look beautiful with black hair.

BRONWYN: Thank you. Your hair's … alright.

MERLE: Bronwyn, your son's lying here with layers of his skin burnt off his face. Thank God he's okay, but he could have died. A spirit should be at rest. There's nothing more haunting than unfinished business.

BRONWYN: *Dhulubang*.

MERLE: My obituaries said that I was born in Tasmania. But I was not. I took my lies to my deathbed. Extremely painful to take secrets like that to your grave.

BRONWYN: I don't want my son to die. How do you pray to your ancestors, Sandy?

SANDY: In whatever way you want. By breathing. Smiling. Laughing. My mother always says the best way to pray is by dancing and singing. *Babbirra*. It means to sing in Wiradjuri. Shall we *babirbambarra*? Sing a song?

BRONWYN: Now?

MERLE: You chant Buddhist chants all the time. I've seen you dong your Buddhist gong.

BRONWYN: I love donging my gong.

SANDY: Do you like dancing, Mrs G? *Waganha?*

BRONWYN: I love to *waganha*.

MERLE: You know where Buddha comes from, Bronwyn?

BRONWYN: Will you dance with me, Sandy?

SANDY: Here?

MERLE: Will you chant with me, Bronwyn?

BRONWYN: You lead.

SANDY: Alright.

MERLE: This was Gandhi's favourite mantra. It was on his lips when he died.

BRONWYN: John's not going to die.

MERLE: Let's chant it to, John.

> SANDY *slow dances with* BRONWYN. MERLE *holds* BRONWYN *from behind.*

Om, Sri Rama Jaya Rama, Jaya, Jaya Rama.

BRONWYN: *Om, Sri Rama Jaya Rama, Jaya, Jaya Rama.*

ALL: *Om, Sri Rama Jaya Rama, Jaya, Jaya Rama.*

SANDY: *Waganha.*

ALL: *Waganha.*

SANDY: *Om, Sri Rama Jaya Rama, Jaya, Jaya Rama.*

> JOHN *sits up suddenly.*

BRONWYN: John!

SANDY: Thank God.

BRONWYN: It's okay, Mummy's here.

JOHN: I feel like a mummy myself.

> ANIL *enters.*

ANIL: Oh, my gods. My brown angel has risen!

SANDY: How could you let this happen, Anil?!

ANIL: I feel so terrible.

SANDY: What actually happened?

ANIL: We were shooting the finale dance scene. It was going perfectly well. Ready to go out with a big bang. Then it did. A packet of Punjabi pyrotechnics prematurely exploded in his face.

SANDY: Don't you have a stunt man for that?

ANIL: Budget cuts.

SANDY: I can't believe no-one was checking health and safety on such a big film set. You should be fined and arrested!

ANIL: I'm sorry, Sandy. I feel responsible. It was my personal 'No H and S Policy' that caused this.

SANDY: We don't do things that way in this country. You've been here long enough. You should have learnt that by now!

ANIL: I'm trying to adapt, mate. It's not easy.

SANDY: You should try harder.

BRONWYN: He's right, Sandy. It's not easy.

JOHN: It's not your fault, Anil.

ANIL: Thank you, John. Fault is useless foreign concept. I take the blame only.

JOHN: What's happening with *Addy*?

ANIL: I didn't dare think about it. I've been feeling terrible. I'm the only Hindu who's ever felt Catholic guilt.

JOHN: Start editing. Did you shoot enough to cut together something for the finale?

ANIL: I did.

JOHN: Well—go and finish your movie!

ANIL: With your blessing?

JOHN: Of course.

ANIL: Thank you, John. I want to premiere this baby on Independence Day in India for the Mumbai Film Festival. We only have a few months. Best get cracking. Rest up, my friend. Because I'm paying for you and your family to fly to India! And I'm going to put you all up in a palace!

> ANIL *exits.*

JOHN: Mum, please tell me the truth. Where are we from?

> *Pause.* MERLE *comforts* BRONWYN.

BRONWYN: I wasn't born in England, John. Neither was your father. I came here in the seventies. From Bombay.

JOHN: Mumbai.

BRONWYN: I'll always remember it as Bombay. Your father and I are … Anglo-Indian. Just like Englebert Humperdinck. Cliff Richard. Merle Oberon.

JOHN: So many lies, Mum. Why?

BRONWYN: When I arrived here, I had a funny accent and people made fun of me. I met your father. He'd experienced the same sort of thing. We wanted to assimilate. We both had white skin. Especially your father, and we decided to … to move on. My mother told me when I was growing up that she was British and her mother did and her mother did too, even though we were all born in India. Same with your father's family. We're a mixture. Once India got back its independence from the British, we struggled. We were all messed up for being mixed up. Colonialism has a lot to answer for.

JOHN: You've got a lot to answer for.

BRONWYN: I do. And I'm being honest with you now, Johnny. Your father and I thought because we were both fair that you would be too. Livvy turned out good. I mean—fair. But sometimes with Anglo-Indians there's a throwback.

JOHN: I'm sorry I'm not the budgerigar you wanted, Mum.

BRONWYN: I wanted you. You're my little boy. I just don't want your children to have the same struggles as we have.

JOHN: Dark blood is strong.

BRONWYN: Yes—it is.

JOHN: I hate you, Mum.

> SANDY *holds* BRONWYN*'s hand.*

SANDY: It wasn't so long ago that you were pretending to be someone else to get by, John. Everyone does it.

JOHN: You haven't.

> *A* DOCTOR *enters.*

DOCTOR: Okay. Time to take these bandages off.

> *The* DOCTOR *carefully removes the bandages.* MERLE *grabs an Obie light and shines its white light on* JOHN*'s face.*

Oh great, the scabs have fallen off.

> JOHN*'s face is very fair under the Obie light. He looks caucasian.*

Wow, you're white. Your skin's turned white.

JOHN: What's wrong with me, doctor?

DOCTOR: There's nothing wrong with you, unless you think there's something wrong with being white? This is amazing. Your skin tissue has healed perfectly under the scabs. But you've lost a fair bit of pigment in your skin. I've got to call the student doctors in to see this.

JOHN: What's going on?

DOCTOR: You're the first brown patient I've had to turn white.

JOHN: I'm hypercolour.

DOCTOR: You're one lucky man, John Green.

BRONWYN: Will this be … permanent?

DOCTOR: Medically, this is rare, but it does happen. After a few months your original skin colour should return. It'll just take some time for the skin cells to repair and for the pigment to grow back. You'll be fine.

JOHN: Will I be okay to go to India for the premiere? For the film festival?

DOCTOR: Mate, you can go to any festival you want. Even Burning Man.

SCENE SEVENTEEN

We hear noises of a busy street in Mumbai. The DOCTOR *becomes* ANIL. JOHN *still has a white face from the Obie light.*

ANIL: Press conference starts in a few minutes. *Jaldi karo*. Get a move on.

JOHN: Sorry we're late.

ANIL: This is Bombay. Traffic is not terrific.

JOHN: Did my family get in okay?

ANIL: Yes. Danno brought a good-looking young Pakistani man with him whom he said was his pen pal. I managed to get an extra press pass for him. They're all cooling down in the palace.

JOHN: You really put everyone up in a palace?

ANIL: No. Palace View Hotel. Two-star. But it has a view of a palace. Partial view. But the palace is palatial. Welcome to India, my friend! Why aren't you wearing your contact lenses like I told you to?

JOHN: I told you, I'm not gonna wear them.

ANIL: It's such a blessing that you look so white and milky now. Bollywood will love you even more. You'll get so much work if you stay here.

JOHN: The doc says that I won't be white for much longer, Anil.

ANIL: *Arrey*, who cares, *yaar*? Milk it for all it's worth.

> PHOTOGRAPHERS *and* PRESS *enter.* JOHN *sits at a long desk with* ANIL. SANDY *sits to the side.*

Subtitles appear on a screen in the theatre when the PRESS PEOPLE *and* JOHN *speak in Hindi.* MERLE *still shines the Obie light on* JOHN.

PRESS PERSON 1: *Critics ne aapki adakaari ki kaafi prashansa kari hai ... par aapke uchcharan ki kaafi khilli bhi udayee hai. Kya aapko nahi lagta ki aapki aawaaz thodi ajeeb hai?*

> *Subtitles:* 'The film critics have praised your acting but find that you have a funny accent. Do you realise that your voice is strange?'

JOHN: *Haan. Ye baat sach hai ki meri aawaaz mai kuch kami hai. Par mujhe ye bhi lagta hai ki hum sabhi apni aawaaz ko hee to dhoondne ki koshish main hai.*

> *Subtitles:* 'Yes. I do. But I think we are all trying to find our own voice, aren't we?'

PRESS PERSON 2: *John ji! John Green to hua aapka ... screen name— Lekin aapka asli naam kya hai?*

> *Subtitles:* 'John Green is obviously your stage name—but what is your original Indian name?'

JOHN: *Mera asli naam hai ... John Green.*

> *Subtitles:* 'My real name is John Green.'

PRESS PERSON 1: *Apke background ko leke logon main tarah ki afwah aur charchain hain. Haal filhaal main ye suna gaya hai ki aap aadhe bharatiya aur aadhe Austrian hain aur aapka janmsthal Austrian Alps hai. Wah kya badiya mishran hai do sanskritiyon ka! Kya aap humain pusht roop se ye bata sakte hain ki asliyat kya hai?*

> *Subtitles:* 'There has been a lot of gossip and speculation about your mixed race heritage. The latest news is that you are half-Indian, half-Austrian, and that you were born in the Austrian alps. How wonderfully exotic! Can you confirm where you are actually from?'

JOHN: *Sahi baat hai ki mere origin ke baare main alag reports hain. Actually mujhe bahut hansi aati hai unko padkar.*

> *Subtitles:* 'Yes, there have been conflicting reports. I find them rather hilarious.'

... Khoon hai. Khoon ka rang wahi hai jo hona chahiye. Aur wo rang hai laal. Zyadatar filmon main, hamari bhi film main, jo nakli khoon istemaal hua hai who nakli hi lagta hai. Chamakta laal rang. Ya yun kahiye, Gulaabi. Asli zindagi mai jab asli khoon behta hai to wo brown hota hai.

> *Subtitles: 'Blood is blood, whether is it mixed or not. And it is red. In most films and even in our film—the fake blood stains look too fake. Too bright. Too pink. In real life when blood stains—it is actually brown.'*

PRESS PERSON 2: *Aap paheliyan kyon bujha rahe hain. Saaf batate kyon nahin ki aap kahan se hain?*

> *Subtitles: 'You haven't answered the question. Where are you actually from?'*

JOHN: *Dekhiye kabhi ... kaale aur safed ke beech ... grey area bhi hota hai ...*

> *Subtitles: 'Sometimes ... in between black and white ... there is a grey area ...'*

... I'm from Greystanes.

> MERLE *switches off the Obie light.*

SCENE EIGHTEEN

LIVVY, BRONWYN, JOHN, SANDY *and* ANIL *stare out at the Taj Mahal.* JOHN*'s face is brown again, without the Obie light.*

JOHN: We made it.

SANDY: The Taj Mahal.

JOHN: The world's most romantic monument of love. Such stunning symmetry.

SANDY: It's the most beautiful sight I've ever seen.

JOHN: You're the most beautiful sight I've ever seen. *Tum bahut sundar ho.*

SANDY: Gawd, I love it when you speak Hindi.

JOHN: *Chalo.* Let's go home.

SANDY: You should stay.

JOHN: I wanna be with you.

SANDY: This is your dream.

JOHN: You're my dream.

> SANDY *laughs.*

Renee emailed me. She offered me another role on 'Bondi Parade'.

SANDY: Another doctor?

JOHN: No. A surf shop owner. I told her I'd take it only if Danno could direct an episode. She agreed. I drive a hard bargain since being over here. You should see me at the fruit market.

LIVVY: Mum and me are—

BRONWYN: Mum and I.

LIVVY: Mum and I are going to buy some toe rings and some anklet jingle-jangle things.

BRONWYN: And a *sari.*

LIVVY: Can we get an auto rickshaw, Mum?

BRONWYN: Of course.

ANIL: Bronwyn, I love your new hairdo. It's great that you've let your grey roots grow back.

BRONWYN: Thank you. I feel young again.

> ANIL *exits to one side of the stage.*

I've come home, Livvy.

LIVVY: Like Lassie?

BRONWYN: Yeah. Let's go drink a lassi, Livvy.

> BRONWYN *and* LIVVY *exit.*

SANDY: Will you come and work with me again when you're not a surf shop owner?

JOHN: Won't you get in trouble?

SANDY: I've been speaking with Gav.

JOHN: What?

SANDY: We're merging our companies. I want you in it. I want my dancers in it. I even want your mate, the Greek Captain Cook.

JOHN: Spyro?

SANDY: Yep, I want to include everyone. I want him.

JOHN: I want you.

SANDY: You've got me. *Tum mera nyiwarri ho.*

JOHN: How did you learn to speak Hindi so quickly?

SANDY: Well, unlike you, I didn't have access to Bollywood's biggest Hindi tutor, so I downloaded Bollywood's Best Pick-Up Lines app … it's hilarious.

JOHN: What's *nyiwarri*? That's not Hindi, is it?

SANDY: It's my Wiradjuri language. I'm mixing Hindi with Wiradjuri.

JOHN: What does it mean?

SANDY: What do you think it means?

JOHN: It means that you love me?

SANDY: Who's a clever convict?

JOHN: Will you teach me the Wiradjuri language, Sandy?

SANDY: Only if you're a good boy, Jolly John. Might have to lock you up for a while and throw away the key so I can stop you dancing ever again.

JOHN: You wouldn't hold me back from dancing, would you?

SANDY: Never. Go on. *Waganha!*

JOHN: You haven't seen my new move yet, have you? The Rainbow Cobra. It's an Aussie-Indian dance. It's lethal.

 MERLE *enters.* JOHN *dances around like a cobra about to strike.*

SANDY: What are you doing?

JOHN: I'm about to break Bollywood's biggest taboo …

SANDY: What's that?

 JOHN *kisses* SANDY. *She kisses him back.*

MERLE: It was never John! The chosen one is *Sandy Gandhi!*

 SANDY *looks to the audience.*

SANDY: Blackout!

 She clicks her fingers and the lights snap to black.

THE END

Bali Padda and Griffin Independent present:

LIGHTEN UP

By NICHOLAS BROWN & SAM McCOOL

Lighten Up opened at the SBW Stables Theatre on 2nd December 2016 and ran until 17th December 2016 as part of Griffin Theatre Company's 2016 independent season.

Producer **BALI PADDA**
Director & Dramaturg **SHANE ANTHONY**
Set & Costume Designer **TOBHIYAH STONE FELLER**
Lighting Designer **CHRISTOPHER PAGE**
Sound Designer & Composer **BUSTY BEATZ**
Stage Manager **LAUREN TULLOH**
Associate Producer (Griffin Theatre Co.) **ESTELLE CONLEY**
Director's Attachment **HANNAH TONKS**
Design Intern **MAELI CHEREL**
Publicist **EMMA JONES**
Publicity Photographer **JOHNNY DIAZ NICOLAIDIS**
Rehearsal Photographer **DUSK DEVI VISION**
Graphic Designers **CLARE MARSHALL, JEFF VAN DE ZANDT, RE:**

With
KATIE BECKETT
NICHOLAS BROWN
VIVIENNE GARRETT
JULIE GOSS
SAM McCOOL
BISHANYIA VINCENT

The production runs for approximately 130 minutes including an interval.

Bali Padda would like to thank the following people without whom the production would not have been possible: Augusta Supple, Adam Majsay, Lenore & Paul Robertson, Gavin Vance, Pearl Tan, Sarah Goodes, Polly Rowe, Rachael Azzopardi, James Evans, Luke Cowling, Suzanne Miller, Kristine Landon-Smith, Sheila Jayadev, Helena Harris, Sharne McGee and all the Griffin staff: Lee Lewis, Ben Winspear, Karen Rodgers, Melanie Carolan, Will Harvey, Aurora Scott, Dino Dimitriadis, Lane Pitcher, Peter O'Connell, Elliott Wilshier, Damien Storer, Maria Dimopulos, Alex Herlihy, Renee Heys, Julian Larnach, Jade da Silva, Linda Popic, Kirby Brierty, Kylie Richards, Tracey Whitby.

GRIFFIN INDEPENDENT

Government Partners

Australian Government

Australia Council for the Arts

NSW GOVERNMENT | Arts NSW

Griffin acknowledges the generosity of the Seaborn, Broughton and Walford Foundation in allowing it the use of the SBW Stables Theatre rent free, less outgoings, since 1986.

Playwrights' Notes

I began writing *Lighten Up* back in 2005 as a way to mitigate the systemic racism that was at play in the entertainment industry. What I'd experienced was never overt, it was always underlying which made it difficult to call out because most people didn't see it, therefore it didn't exist. I set out to do something about it by writing this story. I didn't know of many other writers at the time creating stories about the melting pot of Australia so I set out to break the mould. Today things have changed a great deal but we still have a long way to go. I hope that this play inspires other writers and artists to tell their own stories from their own unique viewpoints and that diversity becomes normality rather than a necessity.

This script helped me to embrace my mixed race heritage and soon I moved to India where a career in Bollywood awaited. I was saddened to see that so many people bleached their skin - the most popular cosmetic there is the Fair & Lovely skin lightening lotion. I thought it was so ridiculous that Australia had an obsession with sun tanning whilst India couldn't get enough of skin bleaching. I knew there was a cross cultural story in this hypocrisy and I was determined to work it into *Lighten Up*.

I became fascinated with my British Indian heritage and the in-between. For the first time, I saw ties between Australia and India as former colonies of England and I finally felt at peace with my Australian Indian heritage. I decided to make my story about an Anglo-Indian man with major identity issues falling in love with an Indigenous Australian woman who helps him come to terms with his skin colour.

In 2012 after several years and many incarnations I approached comedian Sam McCool to co-write the story with me as I knew the play's themes were heavy and that the only way to address this touchy subject was through comedy. *Lighten Up* became a cross cultural comedy and I couldn't be prouder of it and what it stands for.

A long time coming, I hope that *Lighten Up* challenges you, inspires you and above all makes you laugh!

Nicholas Brown
Creator and Co-writer

Writing *Lighten Up* has proved to be an enriching long-term collaboration with an initial stranger of diametric opposites and fundamental similarities who has become a close dear friend. Nicholas Brown had a story he wanted to tell, and I'm proud to have helped him do so. First presented to me as a screenplay with a celebrity attachment, it mutated and morphed through various incarnations to become the deep, complex and comical play it has evolved into.

As a comedian, the vast majority of my writing to date had been by myself for myself to perform. So the immense collaborative effort of writing, developing and performing a stage play has been a tremendous growth experience, where ego dissolves and the play itself becomes the star.

In writing *Lighten Up*, our focus was always on telling an original 'Aussie' story, set amongst the multicultural suburban landscape both Nick and I were raised in, yet one which tackles head-on the complex issues of racism, prejudice, identity, career ambitions, life, the after-life and destiny. We worked tirelessly to imbue all these themes with a powerful sense of humour, absurdity, and a sense of the metaphysical realm beyond our physical human existence. We put our best efforts into avoiding one-dimensional stereotypical characters, and to ensure each character's journey drove the plot, and followed an arc that delivers insightful self-development, learning and lasting change.

The story is essentially a romantic comedy, impacted by the clash of cultures surrounding each character. It highlights the challenges for individuals trying to discover their sense of purpose and true identity in our modern culturally complex world, beyond what we were brought up to believe.

We felt that a powerful way to allow people to access and assess such complex themes was through humour, which we hope tickles our audiences' in performance as much as it bounces off the page to the reader. Please enjoy.

Sam McCool
Co-writer

Director's Note

I was first approached with a working draft for *Lighten Up* over a year ago and I immediately knew I wanted to be involved in helping it arrive on the stage. Not only was I excited by this unique contemporary tale, I was inspired by the relevance of the story given the vibrant dialogue occurring in the Australian entertainment industry surrounding the need for greater diversity on our stages and screens.

Nick and Sam had been working on the project with a variety of collaborators for several years and during this time the project had evolved from a feature film, to a Bollywood musical and finally a stage play.

The draft I read had a lot of ideas, some of which spoke to the different phases of the work's development, others to the desire to say so much about a topic that both Nick and Sam are so passionate about.

To arrive confidently on the stage I felt the work would benefit from a final stage of development before beginning rehearsals. Acting as dramaturg I started to meet with Nick and Sam to discuss the genesis of the idea. I encouraged the team to distill their vision, what they wanted the work to say and what they wanted an audience to take away from the experience of watching the production. Both writers embraced this process with generosity, rigour and a quiet patience.

Over the last two months the creative team and cast have refined the work in an ongoing process of development towards a final production draft. As dramaturg and director I have listened closely to the room, questioning intentions, challenging assumptions, encouraging clarity and ultimately seeking the truth behind the initial idea. I'd love to thank the entire team for tackling such sensitive material with courage and respect.

Shane Anthony
Director & Dramaturg

SHANE ANTHONY
Director & Dramaturg

Shane works as a director in Australia and overseas. Recent directing credits include *The Whale* for Redline Productions at The Old Fitz Theatre, *Songs for the Fallen* at the New York Musical Theatre Festival (Winner of Most Outstanding Show), Sydney Festival, Arts Centre Melbourne, Brisbane International Arts Festival and The Old Fitz, *Pornography* by Simon Stephens for NIDA, *Altar Boyz, Calendar Girls, Avenue Q* for Fortune Theatre (New Zealand), *Doctor Faustus* and *The Crucible* for RCHK (Hong Kong), *Mrs Bang: A Series of Seductions* for the 32nd Stage Song Festival (Poland), *Often I Find That I Am Naked* for Critical Stages – (Australian National Tour), *My Name is Rachel Corrie* for La Boite Theatre, *Orestes, Trojan Women* and *Radio Hysteria* for NIDA Open, *Motortown* for 23rd Productions (Nomination Best Show Matilda Awards). He worked as movement coach on the Australian feature film, *Sleeping Beauty* and in 2009 worked as show director for CIRCA on their European tour of CIRCA '09. In 2007 he travelled to New York to continue training with Anne Bogart and the Saratoga International Theatre Institute in Viewpoints and the Suzuki Method of Actor Training and in 2012 he received a Mike Walsh Fellowship to attend the New York Film Academy. He is a graduate of the Directing Program at the National Institute of Dramatic Art (NIDA, Sydney), Screenwriting for Feature Film at the Australian Film, Television and Radio School and has also completed a BA in Theatre Studies at Queensland University of Technology (QUT).

BUSTY BEATZ
Sound Design & Composer

A killer musical director, brilliant composer, sought after sound designer and powerhouse performer, Busty Beatz creates fearless music and theatre for global audiences. As a Sound Designer and Composer, she has worked with Belvoir St, Sydney Theatre Company, Bell Shakespeare, Theatre Company of South Australia, Queensland Theatre, Powerhouse Youth Theatre and, and La Boite Theatre Company. Musical Direction credits include *East London/West Sydney* for Sydney Festival, Polytoxic's *The Rat Trap* and the award winning show *Briefs*. This beat-making Mama is the Co-Artistic Director of Black Honey Company, with her sister Candy B, creating Fearless Sticky Performance that excites, terrifies and liberates. A production house and consultancy team, they have collaborated for over 15 years to defy the norm and push intersectional feminism centrestage. As the 2016 Company in Residence at La Boite, they aim to decolonise theatre by creating brilliant work featuring Women of Colour. Busty Beatz is currently creating new work *One The Bear* and smashing stereotypes across Europe with theatrical explosion *Hot Brown Honey* - winning the UK's 2016 Total Theatre Award for Innovation, Experimentation and Playing with Form. Alongside creating and performing, Busty Beatz is an infamous DJ leading audiences onto dance floors around the world.

KATIE BECKETT
Sandy

Katie Beckett is on the rise, as an actor and writer. Appearing in TV shows such as *Redfern Now* and *Black Comedy*, film and also many theatre productions. She is the 2015 winner of the Balnaves Award through Belvoir St Theatre. She has also written a play *Which Way Home*, that will be part of the 2017 Sydney Festival playing at Belvoir St with the assistance of Ilbijerri Theatre Company. Film credits include *Little J and Big Cuz*, *The Marshes*, *Talkers*, *Drover's Boy* and *Blackground*. Katie Beckett's stage credits include *Which Way Home*, *Kill the Messenger*, *Coranderrk*, *Onwards and Upwards*, *This Fella*, *My Memory* (Moogahlin Performing Arts); *Impossible Plays*, *Pull My Strings* and *I Will Play for You*, *Wrong Skin* (Next Wave Festival); *Winyaboga* and *To Soothe a Dying Pillow* (Andrea James). She won the Ian Bowie Memorial Award and was shortlisted for the Yvonne Cohen Award for her solo work-in-progress, *Coloured Diggers*, performed at the Dreaming Festival 2009, Museum of Contemporary Art, and the Coloured Diggers ANZAC Day march in Redfern in 2008, 2009 and 2010. She was also successful in gaining a place in the Ilbijerri Writers' Residency.

NICHOLAS BROWN
Co-Writer & John Green

Nicholas Brown is actor, playwright, screenwriter, singer and songwriter. A NIDA graduate, he has had lead roles in the Indian/Bollywood films *Sedition*, *Pratichhaya*, *Love You To Death* and *Kites*. In Australia, Nick has appeared in the films *unINDIAN*, *Random 8*, *A Man's Gotta Do*, *Temptation* and *The Characters*. TV roles include *The Code 2*, *Packed To The Rafters*, *Mr and Mrs Murder*, *The Elegant Gentleman's Guide to Knife Fighting*, *Underbelly Files: The Man Who Got Away*, *Lucky Dragon*, *City Homicide*, *Home and Away*, *The Cooks*, *White Collar Blue* and *Heartbreak High*. Theatre credits include Lumiere in Disney India's *Beauty and the Beast*, Jesus in Alyque Padamsee's *Jesus Christ Superstar* in Mumbai, *Dead Man Brake* (Merrigong Theatre), *The Laramie Project* (Sydney Theatre Company Education), *A Counting And Cracking Of Heads* (CarriageWorks), *Rehaan Engineer's Seven Jewish Children* (Project 88 Art Gallery, Mumbai), *Rehaan Engineer's Doctrine: How to Survive Under Siege* (Kunsten Festival des Arts, Brussels), *Miss Bollywood – The Shilpa Shetty Musical* (Royal Albert Hall, London, UK, and Netherlands and German tour), *The Oresteia, Romeo and Juliet* (representing the NIDA company at the 9th International Drama Schools Festival in Transylvania, Romania), *Fewer Emergencies* (Any Road Productions / Tamarama Rock Surfers), *Spew* (Darlinghurst Theatre) and *Frozen* (B Sharp). His screenwriting credits include *Tantra 2* and the fantasy film *The Brownies*. Nicholas is a proud member of Actors' Equity and the Equity Diversity Committee.

MAELI CHEREL
Design Intern

Maeli spent most of her childhood moving from country to country so it felt only natural to move to a different hemisphere after university. She originally chose Perth for its weather, its wind, and its waves and has now more or less called it home. After a few of years studying and working as an engineer, Maeli decided it was time for a career change. For a number of reasons she chose a path into the Arts industry and applied to study Set and Costume Design at the Western Australian Academy of Performing Arts. She is in the final weeks of completing her first year and is currently designing the set for next year's production of *The Blind Giant is Dancing*. Since starting the course in February, Maeli has had a chance to assist on a number of shows, but is excited to travel to Sydney to assist on *Lighten Up*, her first show outside WAAPA. Maeli can safely say that the decision to shift towards a creative industry has been one of the most satisfying choices she has made.

VIVIENNE GARRETT
Bronwyn

Vivienne is a NIDA graduate who has worked with most major theatre companies in Australia. Vivienne's career spans decades - playing Rose in TV's *No. 96*, roles in *Matlock Police, Division Four, Homicide, The Norman Gunston Show, Mother & Son, Bodyline, Haydaze, Ship to Shore, Streetsmartz* and the award winning series *Minty*. Vivienne won the 1995 Swan Gold Award for *Dead Funny*, and was nominated for best actress and best supporting actress in 2004 and 2010. She won best supporting actress in 2013 for *Other Desert Cities*. Vivienne taught acting at WAAPA - Theatre and Music Theatre courses, Screen Acting at TAFTA and Voice at ECU and FTI. Vivienne has performed two solo shows, *Death of Minnie* and *Witchplay*. Other plays include *The Crucible, The Tempest, As You Like It, Waiting for Godot, The Dybbuk, Measure for Measure, Vagina Monologues, Europe, Black Rock, Top Girls, Checklist for Armed Robber, Equus, Necessary Targets, Mariner, Bedroom Farce, Lebensraum*, as well as *The Clean House* and *When the Rain Stops Falling* for Black Swan Theatre Co in Western Australia. She co-wrote and directed *Breast Stroke* for the stage and for ABC radio National plus 26 short stories. Vivienne is a voice over artist and yoga teacher. Vivienne has been a proud member of Actors' Equity since 1970.

JULIE GOSS
Livvy / Merle / Heather

Julie Goss graduated from NIDA in 2003. Theatre Credits: *Dionyza and Bawd*, *Pericles* directed by John Bell, Bell Shakespeare. Nerissa, *The Merchant Of Venice* National Tour, directed by Anna Volska, Bell Shakespeare. *Actors At Work* National Tour, directed by Marion Potts, Bell Shakespeare. Juliet, *Romeo And Juliet* and Chorus, *The Libation Bearers* directed by Mark Gaal. UNESCO International Theatre Workshops, Sinaia, Romania, *NIDA Devised*, directed by Mark Gaal. *Across The Story Bridge*, written and directed by Sean Hall, NIDA Open. Marika, *Five Times Dizzy*, directed by Des Davies, Theatre South. Julie is a regular Voice Over Artist for ABC'S Media Watch and various campaigns for television and radio. In 2007, Julie was a recipient of the International Actor's Fellowship at Shakespeare's Globe Theatre in London, representing Bell Shakespeare. Julie is a proud member of Actors' Equity.

SAM MCCOOL
Co-Writer & Anil / Guillaume / Mana / Doctor / Indian Press Person 2

Sam McCool is a writer, emcee and stand up comedian who speaks 4 languages and has travelled to over 60 countries. In 2016, he premiered his solo show *Turning Thoughty* on his 40th birthday at the Sydney Opera House and completed a World Tour including shows in Singapore, Kuala Lumpur, Paris, Los Angeles, Las Vegas and at the Rio Olympics. Sam was a finalist on *Australia's Got Talent*, appeared on various TV and radio shows in Australia, an Indonesian soap opera, Aussie feature film *Dags* and created ads for Microsoft. He regularly performs at corporate events for Australia's biggest institutions including 3M, BD, LJH, AMP, CBA, ING, ZIP, TAB, UNSW, OPTUS, ACCOR, DOMAIN, MIRVAC. Eventually he aims to diversify to companies without acronyms. He has performed for organisations as diverse as the Canadian Tourism Commission, Bali International Fashion Show, Macedonian Film Festival, US VFW, Mekong Club, Arab-Australian Business Council, ANZ Business Association of India and Disneyland Paris. Sam has supported worthy causes such as Earth Hour, the Oncology Children's Foundation, RedKite and FSHD. He was invited to help launch the Australian Human Rights Commission Anti-Racism campaign at UNSW with his show *Embracist*. Finally his collaboration with Nicholas Brown has led to the production and publishing of their original play *Lighten Up*.

CHRISTOPHER PAGE
Lighting Designer
Christopher is a theatrical, installation and events lighting designer whose design work has been seen across Sydney, throughout regions of Australia and parts of the world. Chris' recent design credit include: *A Life In The Theatre, A Man With Five Children, Ride & Fourplay* (Darlinghurst Theatre); *4 minutes 12 seconds* (Outhouse Theatre); *E-Baby* (Video), *Betrayal, History of Falling Things, The Good Doctor, Blue/Orange* (Ensemble Theatre); *Journey's End* (ATYP Cameos); *Defying Gravity, Blood Brothers, Do You Hear The People Sing?* (Enda Markey Presents); *The Witches, Five Properties of Chainmale* (Griffin Theatre); *House of Ramon Iglesia, Platonov* (Mop Head); *Black Jesus, His Mother's Voice, Great Expectations* (Bakehouse Theatre); *The Dark Room, Windmill Baby, As You Like It* (Belvoir), *Truck Stop* (Q Theatre) and *Hooting & Howling, Boxing Day* (Critical Stages). Chris' site specific work includes: *Ancient Lives* (MAAS); *El Anatsui* (Carriageworks); *Action Stations* (National Maritime Museum); *Becalmed Heart, Met You in a City That Isn't on a Map* (Underbelly Arts Festival); *Mangroves* (Kate Richards & UNSW) and *Parramasala Festival 2012* (Parramatta City Council).

HANNAH TONKS
Director's Attachment
Hannah first became aware of the Performance Arts in the early nineties in New Zealand where she appeared in a Pampers Nappies print advertisement. From this prestigious beginning she explored her passion for painting, writing and performing. In just over twenty years this passion and dedication for the arts has not faltered. During this time Hannah has painted an award-winning painting, written an award-winning short story, written a musical, directed a musical and has performed in an abundance of independent amateur productions. Hannah aspires to create new Australian works, regardless of whether or not the government values the creative industries.

LAUREN TULLOH
Stage Manager

Lauren's passion is to create the magic of theatre for the audience. As a young girl she was enthralled by many theatrical and musical productions. However, it wasn't until her final year in high school that she discovered her local musical societies. This led to three years of skills development in Stage Management before attending NIDA, completing a Bachelor of Dramatic Art (Production) in 2009. Theatre credits include *The Gruffalo* and *The Gruffalo's Child* for CDP Theatre Producers which toured Australia and New Zealand extensively. Lauren believes she has now seen the back of nearly every theatre in Australia! She also toured *The Gruffalo: Songs from the Show* for Tall Stories UK to Singapore. Lauren then worked at Sydney Opera House for a season of *Charlie and Lola's Extremely New Play*. Returning to musical theatre, Lauren has worked as Stage Manager for *Sunset Boulevard*, *Evita* & *Legally Blonde* with Willoughby Theatre Company. Most recently, Lauren has Stage Managed *Betrayal* at Ensemble Theatre, *Spring Awakening* at ATYP, *The Fantasticks* and *Violet* at Hayes Theatre Co, *Songs For A New World* and *Violet* at Chapel Off Chapel, and is excited to be working with the team of *Lighten Up*.

BISHANYIA VINCENT
Janelle / Gav / Renee / Sydney City Producer / Receptionist / Indian Press Person 2

Bishanyia is a Sydney based actor and voice over artist who moved back to Australia in 2013 after 9 years in the UK. Graduating from The Oxford School of Drama in 2010, her theatre credits include *Where do little birds go?* – Old Fitzroy Theatre, *Harvest* – New Theatre, *Top Girls* – New Theatre, *The Rivals* – UK National Tour and West End, *Private Resistance* – UK National Tour, *After The Fall* – MFS Hampstead Theatre, *Selling Me* – MFS Hampstead Theatre, *The Country Wife* – OSD Theatre, *Time and The Conway's* – OSD Theatre, *Othello* – The Barn Studio, *As You Like It* – Blenheim Palace Gardens Summer Shakespeare, and *The Mother in Law* – OSD Theatre. Bishanyia works regularly in voice over, radio and commercials and has various TV credits including the Emmy award winning comedy series *#7DayLater*. She was also nominated for The Stephen Sondheim Society Student Performer of the Year Awards 2010, and received a commendation for one of her recordings in The BBC Carleton Hobbs Radio Awards 2010.

Production Patrons
Lenore and Paul Robertson

Publishing Patron
Adam Majsay

Production Donors

Pearl Tan
Gavin Vance
Giani Santokh Singh Padda

Ravin Randhawa
Robyn Ayres
Miriam Greenbaum

**We would also like to thank our contributors
to our crowdfunding campaign:**

Adam Majsay
Aileen Huynh
Amanda Bishop
Amanda McGregor
Amanda Rae Kelly
Amy Hume
Ana Tiwary
Ansuya Nathan
Arka Das
Augusta Supple
Belinda Montgomery
Ben Tan
Benjamin John Kuzma
Brendan O'Mahony
Caron Wadick
Casey Donovan
Chris Bowden
Claire Calderwood
Claire Gartrell
Daniel Monks
Darby Minner
Darrin Penola
Dino Dimitriadis
Dipen Rughani
Elena Carapetis
Eloise Snape
Erica Lovell
Eva di Cesare
Fiona Press
Francesca Savige
Gary Paramanathan
Gavin Vance
Gavin Walburgh
Gerard Carroll
Goldele Rayment
Hannah Tonks
Ildiko Susany
James Beach
Jamie Kay
Jeanette Maple
Jennifer Rani
Jennifer Solomon
Jessica Loudon
John Wonnacott
Jono Gavin
Joy Hopwood
Joy Tulloh
Karee Gurtman
Karen Majsay & Nick Flynn
Karen McIvor
Kathryn Courtney Prior
Keith Agius
Kenny Douglas
Kerri Lock & Douglas Hemingway
Khushrukh Pai

Kristine Landon-Smith
Lauren Clair & Curly Fernandez
Laurinda Harch
Lenore & Paul Robertson
Leigh Scully
Liam Kemp
Linus Karsai
Lisa Freshwater
Luke Carson
Mala Ghedia
Margaret Lowe
Margarita Adams
Mark Dessaix
Michael Gupta
Michelle Favero
Michelle Hourigan
Mike Beder
Miriam Spry
Natasha Kaminski
Natasha Marie
Nigel Giles
Nisrine Amine
Patrick McIntyre
Prasanna Pichai
Prudence Holloway
Queenie van de Zandt
Rebecca Lee
Rebecca Rocheford Davies
Shay Spencer
Sandra Eldridge
Sean Hall
Sharon Johal
Shaun Parker
Shaun Rennie
Sheila Jayadev
Sheridan Harbridge
Sian Taryn Ewers
Sonya Suares
Stephanie Kelly
Szabolcs & Margaret Majsay
Talis Graudins
Tara O'Sullivan
Thushy Sathiamoorthy
Tina McFay
Tina Mitchell
Tracey Brown
Vanessa Hyde
Victoria White Davies
Virginia Gay
Vitas Varnas
Waseem Khan
Yalin Ozucelik & Lizzie Schebesta
Zenia Starr
Anonymous x 3

BALI PADDA
ACTOR I PRODUCER I DIVERSITY
www.balipadda.com

Bali is an actor and producer who is a passionate advocate for diversity in the Australian arts and cultural sector. A champion of diverse representation on stage and screen, Bali works extensively to advocate for culturally and linguistically diverse communities in mainstream media.

Bali sits on the MEAA National Performers' Committee, the elected panel of professional actors that represent actors on industrial matters, and is the Co-Chair of the Equity Diversity Committee, a panel of professional performers established to advocate for and realise the principles of diverse casting and employment, and address the overriding issues about the lack of diversity and inclusion in Australian performing arts.

His international credits include performing in a British-Brazilian co-production at the Young Vic Theatre in London, followed by a critically acclaimed season of *STOMP's Lost & Found Orchestra* at the Royal Festival Hall, London. Since moving back to Sydney in 2009, he has performed both principal and supporting roles on the stage in *Legally Blonde the Musical* (The Concourse), *The Big Funk* (TAP Gallery), *Babies Proms: Bollywood Baby, Oneness: Voice Without Form* (Sydney Opera House), *Singled Out* (Seymour Centre), *The Lunch Hour* (Darlinghurst Theatre with Siren Theatre Co) and *In the Space Between* (Cleveland St Theatre). On the screen, Bali played the lead role in the award-winning short *Letters Home*, as well as featuring in roles in *unINDIAN, Legally Brown* (SBS) and various TV commercials.

In 2016, Bali joins the Season 2 cast of the award-winning *Top of the Lake*, working alongside Elisabeth Moss, David Wenham and Gwendoline Christie under the guidance of Jane Campion. Also, fulfilling his passion of engaging youth with the arts and in regional communities, Bali was Monkey Baa Theatre Co.'s Teaching Artist for NSW, WA & SA for their 2016 tour of *The Peasant Prince*, the story of Mao's Last Dancer, Li Cunxin.

In 2015, Bali was a Finalist as Young Professional of the Year for the India Australia Business & Community Awards, recognising his endeavours to ensure diversity and inclusion becomes a strong focus for the arts & entertainment industry.

Producer credits —
2017	*Sunderella* by Kunal Mirchandani with Trikone Australasia
2016	*Lighten Up* by Nicholas Brown & Sam McCool with Griffin Independent
	Hats Off! For Harmony with Oz Showbiz Cares / Equity Fights AIDS Inc.
2015	*Hats Off! To the Hits* with Oz Showbiz Cares / Equity Fights AIDS Inc.
2014	*Minority Box* (Online, Factual) by Pearl Tan with Pearly Productions
	Equity75 — A toast to Equity by Jonathan Mill with The Equity Foundation
2011	*In the Space Between* by Kunal Mirchandani with Trikone Australasia